Spirit of England

JERROLD NORTHROP MOORE

Spirit Of England

Edward Elgar
in his World

HEINEMANN : LONDON

William Heinemann Ltd,
10 Upper Grosvenor Street, London W1X 9PA

LONDON MELBOURNE TORONTO
JOHANNESBURG AUCKLAND

© Jerrold Northrop Moore 1984
First published 1984
434 47541 6

Phototypeset by Wyvern Typesetting Ltd, Bristol
Printed and bound in Great Britain by
Billings Limited, Worcester

For Malcolm

Contents

Acknowledgements

The author and the publishers wish particularly to acknowledge the courtesy of owners of previously unpublished photographs appearing in this book for the first time: Mrs. Vernon Barran for her photograph of Rosa Burley; Mrs. Mary Fraser for the fine portrait photograph of her father, A. J. Jaeger; and E. Wulstan Atkins for his photograph of his father with Elgar at the Gloucester Festival of 1922.

Grateful thanks are due to several copyright holders for the use of brief quotations here reproduced: first and foremost, to the Trustees of the Elgar Will Trust for permission to reproduce manuscripts and quote from writings both of Sir Edward Elgar of Carice Elgar Blake; to the Trustees of the British Museum, the Governors and Guardians of the National Gallery of Ireland and the Royal Academy of Dramatic Art for the sentences of George Bernard Shaw; to Mrs. I. M. Fresson for quotations from *Edward Elgar: the record of a friendship* by Rosa Burley and Frank C. Carruthers; to Isabella Wallich for the quotation from Fred Gaisberg's diary; to Messrs. J. M. Dent for sentences from W. H. Reed's *Elgar*, Victor Gollancz for extracts from Reed's *Elgar as I Knew Him*, and Hutchinson for the lines from Mary Anderson de Navarro's *A Few More Memories*.

Preface

Why read the life of a creative artist? I have asked myself the question many times – even after beginning to write about Elgar years ago. The composer presumably creates his music to reach as many people as possible. Certainly his success or failure is judged very much on that basis. Above all it is judged on the ability to reach people beyond his own time and place. If the music succeeds, by that token it needs no explication.

Yet the raw material of art is life's experience. Many an artist like Elgar draws deep inspiration from the world around him. Elgar died fifty years ago. Since then we have had a Second World War, the harnessing of atomic power, plastics – a thousand things which change the texture of daily existence. If we go farther back, to Elgar's most fertile years, we go back to the antediluvian world of England in 1900 – the British Empire, the harshest contrasts of city rich and city poor, the deep peace of the Victorian countryside without motor cars – without telephones – without radio – without television – without cinema.

What has that world to say to us? It has two messages, so it seems to me. One is to suggest, in the light of what has happened since, how the seeds of that time have germinated and, by extension, what we might look for in the seeds of our own time. The other is the continuity of human feeling which makes it so. As Elgar's contemporary and fellow Worcestershireman A. E. Housman wrote:

> Then, 'twas before my time, the Roman
> At yonder heaving hill would stare:
> The blood that warms an English yeoman,
> The thoughts that hurt him, they were there.

The life of a creative artist is basically a generous life. He finds the things within him that concern us all, and weaves them in patterns of subtlety and grace to inspire us with new perceptions of ourselves and each other and the world we share. The life which made such music has a further significance – not beyond the music, but beside it. It is the story of a man who gave everything he had to make the world a richer and more understandable place for us.

To tell this story it is not necessary to recall every small detail, every foible and failing which may happen to have been recorded. As Elgar's friend Bernard Shaw once said, an artist has the right to have *his* chain tested by its *strongest* link. Our theme, then, is the finding of patterns – of forms which give understanding to raw existence. That 'inventing' – in the literal meaning of 'coming upon' – is the real subject of the book which follows.

All of Elgar's friends who used to talk to me about him agreed that he was a complex man. But they also agreed that he had extraordinary magnetism. The magnetism was partly made of traits appearing again and again, but in endless ramifications. It is exactly the combination a great artist needs – a recognisable inventory of personal characteristics, which can be woven together in a close-textured fabric of self-expression: in short, a personal style. To emphasise this thematic developmental character, I have set out what seem to me the fundamental matters of Elgar's life one by one. Within each chapter is a degree of chronology. But the main interest here is pattern – pattern which time and place imposed on Elgar, pattern which he fought for and invented within himself.

JNM

Chronology

1857 – Born at Broadheath, near Worcester, 2 June.

1859 – Elgar family returned to live in Worcester.

1863 – Family moved to rooms above W. H. Elgar's music shop at 10, High Street, Worcester. Here Edward lived with his family until 1879.

1863–5 – First schooling at Miss Walsh's School, Britannia Square; piano lessons.

1864 – Death of elder brother Harry at the age of 15 from scarlet fever.

1865–8 – School at Spetchley Park.

1866 – Death of Jo Elgar, 'the Beethoven of the family' at the age of 7 from tuberculosis. Edward heard his first Three Choirs Festival rehearsal: Beethoven's *Mass in C.*

1868–72 – School at Francis Reeve's Academy, Littleton House, Lower Wick.

1869 – Three Choirs Festival rehearsal of *Messiah* inspired Edward to learn the violin.

1869–71 – Music for the children's play (later orchestrated as *The Wand of Youth* Suites 1 and 2).

1872 – Played organ for first full service at St.George's Roman Catholic Church, Worcester.

1872–3 – Apprentice in William Allen's law office.

1873 – Shop assistant in father's music business, began giving violin lessons.

1878 – First played in Three Choirs Festival Orchestra. Attempt to model a Symphony after Mozart's G minor.

1879–84 – Conductor at Powick Lunatic Asylum.

1883 – Visit to Leipzig; engagement to Helen Weaver.

1884 – Engagement broken. *Sevillana* performed at the Crystal Palace.

1886 – Accepted Caroline Alice Roberts as pupil.

1887–9 – Organist at St. George's Church.

1888 – *Salut d'amour* written as engagement present to Alice Roberts.

1889 – Married to Alice Roberts (born 1848) at Brompton Oratory, London.

1889–91 – Residence in London.

1890 – *Froissart* Overture. Birth of only child, Carice Irene.

1891–9 – Living at Forli, Alexandra Road, Malvern Link, Worcestershire. Teaching violin to school and private pupils in the district.

1892 – Finished Serenade for Strings and *The Black Knight* from sketches. First trip to Bavarian Highlands and Bayreuth.

1894 – *Sursum Corda.*

1895 – *Scenes from the Bavarian Highlands*; Organ Sonata.

1896 – *The Light of Life (Lux Christi); Scenes from the Saga of King Olaf.*

1897 – *Imperial March; The Banner of St. George.*

1897–8 – *Caractacus.*

1898–1903 – Tenancy of Birchwood Lodge as a summer retreat.

1898–9 – *'Enigma' Variations.*

1899–1904 – Living at Craeg Lea, Wells Road, Malvern.

1899 – *Sea Pictures.*

1900 – *The Dream of Gerontius.* Took up cycling.

1901 – *Cockaigne* Overture; *Pomp and Circumstance* Marches Nos. 1 and 2.

1902 – *Coronation Ode.*

1902–3 – *The Apostles.*

1903–4 – First visit to Italy.

1904 – *In the South,* first performed in three-day Elgar Festival at Covent Garden, London; *Pomp and Circumstance* March No.3.

1904–11 – Living at Plas Gwyn, Vineyard Road, Hereford.

1904–8 – Professor of Music at the University of Birmingham.

1905 – *Introduction and Allegro.*

1905–11 – Visits to the United States.

1905–6 – *The Kingdom.*

1907 – *Pomp and Circumstance* March No.4; Part songs written in Italy.

1907–8 – *The Wand of Youth* Suites 1 and 2 realised from old children's play music; Symphony No. 1.

1910 – Violin Concerto.

1911 – Symphony No. 2; *Coronation March* and Offertory.

1912–21 – Living at Severn House, 42 Netherhall Gardens, Hampstead, London, N.W.3.

1912 – *The Crown of India; The Music Makers.*

1913 – *Falstaff.*

1914 – Part songs. First gramophone recording. Outbreak of First World War. *Carillon.*

1915 – *The Starlight Express* incidental music.

1915–17 – *The Spirit of England.*

1917 – *The Sanguine Fan; The Fringes of the Fleet.*

1917–21 – Tenancy of Brinkwells, near Fittleworth, Sussex.

1918 – Violin Sonata; String Quartet.

1918–19 – Piano Quintet; Cello Concerto.

1920 – Death of Alice Elgar.

1921–9 – London residence in a flat at 37, St. James's Place.

1923 – *Arthur* incidental music.

1923–7 – Living at Napleton Grange, Kempsey, near Worcester.

1927–8 – Living at Battenhall Manor, Worcester.

1928–9 – Living at Tiddington House, near Stratford-upon-Avon.

1929–34 – Living at Marl Bank, Rainbow Hill, Worcester.

1930 – *Severn Suite; Pomp and Circumstance* March No.5; *Nursery Suite.*

1931 – Opened EMI studios at Abbey Road, London, by conducting the first gramophone recording of *Falstaff.*

1932 – Beginning work on opera, *The Spanish Lady*; Violin Concerto recording with 16-year-old Yehudi Menuhin.

1932–3 – Work on Symphony No. 3.

1934 – Death at Marl Bank, Worcester, 23 February.

1

Elgar and his family

EDWARD ELGAR was a son of the middle class, and many of its ideals guided him through his life. His father, William Henry Elgar (1821–1906), came from Dover, where the sea and Channel piloting were part of the family tradition. But music was also in the family: as boys, both William and his younger brother Henry were taught to play keyboard instruments by a local organist. Music determined William's profession, for when he was old enough to be apprenticed he was sent to the piano firm of Coventry & Hollier in London to learn the craft of tuning. In due course the firm sent him to be their representative in the city of Worcester, 120 miles northwest of London.

Worcester was a Cathedral city, built high along the eastern bank of the Severn to give protection from winter and spring floods. Surrounded by farms and orchards, Worcester had been touched only lightly by the Industrial Revolution, and the main industry of the place was glove-making. There was also the famous porcelain factory. The city buildings were a mixture of newer and older. There were echoes of medieval life not only round the Cathedral, but in the last traces of the old city walls then still remaining. The streets showed Elizabethan half-timbering and Georgian brick. From its loyalty to Charles I and Charles II at the time of the Civil War, Worcester was known as 'the faithful city'.

It was a personable and presentable young man who arrived there in 1841. Several piano tuners were already established, but W. H. Elgar had been sent by his firm especially to tune the instruments at Witley Court, a vast house lying a few miles northwest of the city. Witley Court was the seat of the Earl of Dudley. When William arrived, it was let to the Dowager Queen Adelaide, widow of William IV. The young man tuned the Queen's pianos, and advertised the royal connection for many years afterward on his letterhead. From it he was able to build up a fashionable clientele among the country house owners round Worcester and the gentry and clergy living in the city.

In addition to his keyboard skills, W. H. Elgar was a fair violinist, and so found a place in the musical groups which flourished all over Worcester to provide a focus for neighbourly and social life as well as culture in the city. In the Worcester Glee Club (a vocal meeting with frequent instrumental additions) W. H. Elgar became friendly with two brothers from a family named Leicester.

**Worcester Cathedral and surroundings
from the western bank of the Severn.**

The Leicesters were Roman Catholic, attending regularly at St. George's Church which had been built by the Jesuits soon after Catholic Emancipation in 1829. The Worcester Catholics were in need of an organist, and young Elgar could increase his earnings by taking the job. It entailed training the choir, selecting music in consultation with the priest in charge, the organist occasionally arranging and even writing some of the music himself. W. H. Elgar was a free-thinker, and he wrote to his family in Dover of 'the playhouse mummery of the Papist'. But he took the job, and was to fill it for thirty-seven years.

William Henry Elgar in his fifties, *c.* 1875.

He had need of extra money then, for he courted the sister of the Greenings, with whom he lodged. Ann Greening, whom he married in January 1848, was a few months younger than William, the youngest child of a yeoman farmer (as Elgar's daughter described him for me: a farmer who owned his farm). She was a great reader, and also wrote verses of her own. These she often copied into the pages of scrapbooks side by side with special passages from favourite authors. She loved tales of masculine chivalry and feminine honour: 'she verily believed' (her daughter was to write of her) 'these shadowy forms to be portraits of the people whom she would one day meet with in the world'.

Most of all she enjoyed communing with nature in daily walks at all seasons. She sought the example of the natural world for, as her daughter wrote, 'she loved an atmosphere peaceful yet glowing and vibrating with her own emotions'. Perhaps she was an escapist. Yet she was practical enough to secure her wishes for the children who soon began to appear: when her husband would not buy a cradle, she put rockers on a washing basket, so that her baby could have the reassuring pulse-movement of rocking from side to side.

The children developed in different ways. Harry, the eldest, had his dream fixed on a career of science or medicine before his early death. Lucy, a frustrated intellectual, married a charming man beneath her in every way. She was remembered by friends of mine in Worcester as frumpish, difficult to converse with because of her deafness as an older woman, and isolated by a childless marriage. Yet her skills of observation and memory, shown in her narrative of her brother's childhood, have given us perhaps the most vivid and valuable picture we possess of any great composer's childhood.

The next sister, Pollie, was everybody's favourite. Her charm and humour and intelligence made her the closest of all the brothers and sisters to their mother. And Pollie passed these qualities to her own children and grandchildren to an astonishing degree. She was one of those people whom life could not upset, her sense of balance coming not from placidity but from her warm intelligence.

The elder children had been born in a terraced old house facing the east end of Worcester Cathedral. It made a convenient base for W. H. Elgar to operate his business as a travelling piano tuner. But in 1856 he yielded to his wife's entreaties that their children should be raised in the country, even as she herself had been. They found a remote cottage at Broadheath, a hamlet between three and four miles northwest of Worcester in gently rolling countryside surrounded by farms, woods, and little streams, and with the North Hill of the Malverns just in sight.

The muddy roads of winter and spring made Broadheath inconvenient for W. H. Elgar, who had to lodge in the city and elsewhere many nights in the week. But he made up for that by bringing his musical friends for impromptu concerts to the tiny cottage at weekends. They had a repertory of songs, glees, and instrumental pieces, and the children were allowed to listen often enough to develop their own favourites. One of these was 'Di provenza il mar' from Verdi's recent opera *La traviata*, as sung by William Allen, who on weekdays was a solicitor. Allen was a devout Catholic, and one of his clients was St. George's Church itself, just across the street from his office.

Here was another theme in the family's life. Out of her husband's employment at the Catholic Church, Ann Elgar had formed a theological focus for her own aspirations. In the early 1850s she had gone to the Superior at St. George's and received instruction in the Roman faith. It was a brave decision in an English Cathedral city of that day to turn away from the established church. But Ann never wavered, and brought up all her children as Catholics despite her husband's tacit opposition. The parents in the early years of their marriage made a reasonable job of bridging their differences, and the cottage home at Broadheath was a happy one for their children.

'The Firs' cottage at Broadheath, from a drawing by Buckler, 1856: W. H. and Ann Elgar with Lucy on the central path, Harry by the tree at right, Pollie with the nurse in the doorway.

Edward, the second son and fourth surviving child, came into the family on 2 June 1857 at Broadheath – a day of fine summer weather, as 5-year-old Lucy recalled it. Thus in the baby's immediate surroundings were many of the experiences which would shape his life and art: the world of nature, musical and literary interests on the part of the parents, the formal religion of the one and questioning spirit of the other.

Had the world at Broadheath continued uninterrupted for Edward, its satisfactions might well have sunk any questions, and the creative spirit remained dormant. But in 1859, around the time of his second birthday, a decision was taken to move the family back to Worcester: it would be more convenient for the father's business, and the fifth child now expected would crowd impossibly the tiny cottage at Broadheath. For all the other Elgar children, then, the city of Worcester provided the home either returned to or born into. Edward remained the only child born at Broadheath. And he was to be the only genius.

Back in Worcester, in other rented houses near the Cathedral, the family's younger children appeared – Frederick Joseph in 1859, Francis Thomas in 1862, Helen Agnes at the beginning of 1864. The family were never afterwards to leave the city, which provided the background for all the children's lives henceforth to maturity.

Early in the 1860s W. H. Elgar's friends the Leicesters persuaded him to take a shop in the Worcester High Street for the sale of pianos and music, and soon afterwards he moved his family into the rooms above the shop. These rooms were to remain the permanent family home. Elgar senior cultivated a courtly manner in his profession. He was not so attentive to business as could be wished by his younger brother Henry (who had recently joined the firm). Yet the expansion to music selling brought one clear benefit. Through his friendship with the Cathedral organist and the lay clerks W. H. Elgar secured the agency for selling music to the Cathedral choir.

Edward remembered being taken into the Cathedral from the time he was 4. He kept a lifelong familiarity with the whole building and its monuments – including one horrific old funerary commemoration of a jawless skull surmounting the wings of death. He played among the tombs outside the Cathedral from the time he could walk. He came to know the Cathedral lay clerks as family friends of his parents' home. Yet on every Sunday and holy day he was taken not to the Cathedral or any of the parish churches close by, but half a mile north to the Catholic Church where his mother worshipped and his father played the organ.

By now his father openly detested the rhetoric of priests. Neighbours heard him threatening to shoot his daughters if he caught them going to confession. But it was all noise and bluff: his wife went quietly on her way, using her tact and kindness to reconcile her husband to raising and educating all the children as Catholics. She had her way in everything by means of gentle assurance. In later years Edward acknowledged

**The earliest known photograph of Edward Elgar,
with his mother, *c.* 1859.**

openly that his mother was the great and shaping influence of his life: 'the things she told me', he said, 'I have tried to carry out in my music'.

In the family rooms over the High Street shop two Elgar sons died in Edward's early childhood – the eldest, Harry, of scarlet fever in the spring of 1864, in 1866 Edward's next younger brother 'Jo', of whom he was particularly fond. With Harry's disappearance, Edward became the eldest son just before his seventh birthday. Jo's death two years later removed an enigmatic figure – a child whose precocity in music had gained him the nickname 'the Beethoven of the family'.

Little Jo died too early for more than outlines to be remembered, but they are bold. He had, as Lucy recalled, 'very remarkable aptitude for music in every way from the time he could sit up in his chair'; a concomitant speech defect, and possibly a difficulty with walking as well – 'curiously undeveloped in many ways' was Hubert Leicester's recollection. Jo was the object of his elder brother Edward's deepest affection up to the time of his death when he was 7 and Edward 9.

Jo Elgar (1859–66), 'the Beethoven of the family', with Edward, *c.* 1864.

The youngest son, Frank, shared Jo's musical abilities, and his talent as an oboist and bandmaster were recognised wherever he showed them. But he was beset by what Hubert Leicester saw as a sort of lethargy which he could never shake off. Ultimately he was his father's son and took over the High Street music business. He died a depressed and disappointed man, having experienced the desolation of watching two of his three children fall victim to the family scourge, tuberculosis.

The youngest sister, Helen (nicknamed 'Dot') kept house for her parents. After her mother's death she became a Dominican nun, and rose to be elected Mother General of her Order in England. She combined some of the best qualities of her sister Pollie and her famous brother Edward.

Edward shared his mother's interest in reading. From the time he had been a baby, Ann Elgar had read to the children and told them stories, sometimes of her own invention. In Worcester she was always in and out of bookshops, and the family rooms above the music shop overflowed with books. Edward quickly learnt his mother's way of escaping through the literary imagination. He once said that literature was his first love, and that music had come only as a sort of second choice.

There was more to it than that. Undoubtedly the boy was closer to his mother than his father, but from earliest childhood he had shown the desire and the will to teach himself whatever he wanted to know. His mother was so skilled a teacher that any pursuit fully shared with her must offer little scope to self-teaching. Music was different. His mother enjoyed music but was no practitioner. And his father had shown an early impatience with teaching his children. As he surveyed his son's growing musical skill, W. H. Elgar felt a mixture of pride and jealousy.

At the age of 4 or 5 Edward sat one day at the back of the music shop trying to draw a stave. The stave had only four lines. His father happened to look over his shoulder, and perhaps jumped to the conclusion that the Catholics were influencing even his son's music, as the Gregorian stave consists of four lines: 'What are you doing there, you silly boy?', he asked gruffly. 'Writing music,' was the child's reply. 'Well, don't you know that the proper stave has five lines, not four lines?' That response may have been prompted also by some annoyance at his little son's precocity in the one field in which his wife's competence had left her husband unquestioned supremacy. W. H. Elgar was to live well into the years of his son's fame; practically up to the time of Edward's knighthood the old man would not admit that his elder surviving son had a more than average competence in music. Yet in the early days the father could be proud of Edward too. When the boy quickly gained skill in extemporising at the piano, W. H. Elgar used to take him round to his influential clients and get him to display his skill – for all the world like some small and local Mozart.

The effect of these wealthy and comfortable homes upon the boy who was growing up in rooms over the music shop was profound. A modern child might have reacted jealously, and wished to destroy that superiority. Edward, a true child of his era, reacted by wishing to join it. The latter half of the nineteenth century was a crossroads in English social thought and feeling. On the one hand, it was still just possible to believe in the virtue of the aristocracy – to think that they were entitled to their inherited wealth and position by true superiority. On the other hand, there were the self-help stories of Samuel Smiles and a host of others, showing over and over again how virtue and keenness could raise individuals from rags to riches to join the good people at the top. Both viewpoints were in the teaching of his mother, and her strengths enabled her son to put them together. They made an equation, however subconscious, which was to be one of the guiding principles of Edward Elgar's creative life: that the successful practice of music was bound up with a superior and more comfortable way of life. In that way too, music offered the supreme escape.

The outstanding manifestation of music-making in Worcester was the Three Choirs Festival, rotating year by year among the cathedral cities of Worcester, Hereford, and Gloucester. Chorus and orchestra were drawn from the widest social spectrum, and ticket prices ensured that only the wealthiest citizens and the most prominent gentry occupied the best seats. W. H. Elgar was in the orchestra, and beginning in 1866 he obtained permission for Edward to attend the final combined rehearsal of the week's music.

Edward followed his father into music-making of all kinds through the city. At St. George's Church he learnt to play the organ well enough to be able to deputise from the age of 15 when his father wished to be elsewhere. When years later the old man's irascibility became too much for the choir, Edward actually took over the organistship for two years, but disliked the limitations inherent in the life of a church musician.

He was better pleased with the instrumental ensembles and local orchestras he entered with his father when his violin playing had developed sufficiently. And from 1878 he was in the orchestra recruited for the Three Choirs Festival – at first beside his father in the second violins, but soon amongst the firsts.

Edward's education was entirely at Catholic schools in and around Worcester, finishing at Littleton House across the river at Lower Wick when he was 15. He wanted only to be a musician, and said to his mother that he would not rest until he received a letter addressed 'Edward Elgar, England'. His parents, well knowing the hazards of the music trade, arranged instead a sort of apprenticeship for him with the Catholic solicitor William Allen. Edward made good use of his quickness, and the solicitor characterised him as 'a bright lad'. But the office already had one young favourite securely installed. Edward felt his own abilities were being ignored, and begged to be released. After a year the parents reluctantly agreed, on condition he help in the shop with the accounts.

Elgar Brothers' Music Shop, No. 10 High Street, Worcester,
c. **1910.**

The surviving Elgar children, *c.* 1877: (*foreground:*) Edward (1857–1934) with Tip; Susannah Mary, or 'Pollie' (1854–1936); (*top, left to right*) Helen Agnes ('Dot') (1864–1939); Lucy (1852–1925); Frank (1862–1928).

Soon Edward Elgar began to scrape his living as a violinist and teacher – using the front room over the shop as a studio but also travelling many miles by rail and occasionally on horseback. That was his means of transport to the County Lunatic Asylum at Powick, where in 1879 he won the job of conducting an orchestra of attendants once a week for concerts and dances to divert and edify the patients. Music therapy was in its infancy then. In later years Elgar more than once demolished a pompous interlocutor by beginning a remark: 'When I was at the Lunatic Asylum . . .'

He arranged and wrote music for the Asylum. He wrote songs for the Glee Club and anthems for the Catholic Church choir. During the long sermons there he wrote music for a woodwind quintet formed with friends. He joined a concert orchestra in Birmingham and wrote occasional pieces to be played by them. One or two were performed in London. But it was not until he married at the age of nearly 32, sixteen years after his entry into the musical profession, that he was able to write anything of lasting importance.

This slow and late creative development can be explained partly by self-teaching and the need to find his own way. But self-teaching did not suffice until it was supported by a secure marriage. The proof is in the chronology of his music's appearance. His first important work emerged a year after the marriage. His last, three decades later, came a few months before his wife's death in 1920. The fourteen years of life left to Elgar as a widower produced little more than his bachelor years. For a creative man, Elgar was deeply dependent on his intimates; and first among these without question came his wife.

It has been said that every man seeks a reincarnation of his mother in marriage, and that was certainly true of Elgar. The lady of his choice was older than himself by nearly nine years. She was a writer, having published (at her own expense) a two-volume novel, a long poem, and smaller works. She was gentle and assured of manner. That came partly from her family background: she was in fact many steps higher on the social ladder than the Elgars, for her father had been a Major-General in India, and she lived with her widowed mother in a large house in the countryside south of Malvern, the spa town near Worcester which yielded so many of young Elgar's pupils. Music teaching accounted for the introduction of Miss Caroline Alice Roberts, who applied to Mr. Edward Elgar in the autumn of 1886 for lessons in piano accompaniment.

That winter he set to music one of her poems, *The Wind at Dawn*, showing the wind as an agent for clearing the clouds and permitting the sun to shine in fullest glory. Though Miss Roberts's poem had been written before she met the young music teacher, it could be read as an ideal symbolism of the relationship both were seeking. To Alice, the

Caroline Alice Roberts (1848–1920), *c.* **1885.**

romantically dark young man, full of unrealised creative dreams at the age of 30, offered an ideal focus for her own unrealised dreams. To Edward, this daughter of the upper classes offered a feminine encouragement he had not so far met with outside the relationship with his mother. His love for a young girl in Worcester had ended three years earlier in a broken engagement. With Alice Roberts there was no fear of that.

Neither family was keen on the match. Edward's parents wondered how a woman of 40 could give him romantic fulfilment. She was of a far higher class, and all her friends would look down on him even if she did not herself. And for Ann Elgar, there was the fact that Miss Roberts was Anglican; though this objection was overcome by Alice's enthusiastic conversion to Roman Catholicism soon after the marriage. Alice's parents by this time were dead, but her aunts were horrified at the prospect of this misalliance to a tradesman's son – in their view a mountebank fiddler of no fortune and uncertain temper who would be sure to lead Alice a difficult life. And so he did. But each found in the other an extraordinary fulfilment.

For Alice the fulfilment lay in marriage with a younger man of creative abilities far beyond her own. She never showed the slightest jealousy, and unhesitatingly sank her lesser talent under the rubric: 'The care of a genius is enough of a life work for any woman.' And she had the ultimate satisfaction of knowing that her presence, gentle encouragement, and dog-like devotion in the face of all his moods were absolutely essential to the music of her man. In an age less obsessed than ours with sex, she encouraged his friendships with the younger women of his acquaintance – whom she also befriended.* No wife in any age would do that without the knowledge of some ultimate control. Alice's certainty was that when it came to realising his music, he would have to come to her: she held the assurance he needed, and with it she could simply wind up the string. Yet she would never be cruel enough to do this in any obvious way. As one of the younger women said: 'Hers was truly a great love.'

---

*Despite the obvious wishes of some of the younger women, not a shred of real evidence has ever come my way to show that Elgar's part in any extramarital relationship went beyond friendship. Speculation is idle, for it can only reflect the wishes of the speculator. In the case of a creative artist it is doubly idle, because the entire reason for interesting ourselves in such a life is precisely that life's difference from our own – its production of works of art. No doubt Elgar had private dreams, as we all have, and these are irrecoverable: no biographer, however deep his study, can legitimately claim to be party to those. The biographer's real task is to marshal the artist's experience pre-eminently as he himself has recorded it for us in his life's most important statements – his works.

For Elgar the love was different. It was a love of dependence, with all the self-doubts and frustrations attendant. The same friend, observing them together, said that they appeared to be almost of two different generations – her motherly pride sometimes evoking an almost childish impatience in him. Yet in his heart he knew that her extravagant faith – her silent expectations and demands – were his only final defence against the laziness we all feel, and against the cankerous insecurity which would otherwise have silenced him.

She had braved ostracism from her family, religion, and social class to marry him. She devoted her small income to protecting him from the frustrations of workaday employment as well as she could. She saw to it that his every comfort was catered for in the long succession of houses to which his questing spirit moved them one after another. The usual drill of a removal was for Alice to send Edward to divert himself with friends or at a club in London while she supervised all the packing up and unpacking in the new house. Thus within a few days he could walk into the new home fully settled and equipped. She bore with late nights and early mornings, with more than occasional nervous rudeness to herself and her friends, with a mercurial temper which kept her emotionally overstretched throughout their thirty years together – because she realised that her life's fulfilment was in ministering to this man and his creative spirit.

He returned her love in his own way – in the realisation that no one else would ever have done so much, and that without such extraordinary demonstrations of faith and loyalty his genius would never have been brought to flower and fruit. It was a remarkable marriage, far indeed from the common path. But then so were the partners themselves. In their fears and frustrations we can recognise the links with ourselves; it is the successful creative achievement that sets them apart, and that fact ultimately answers all lesser questions.

In the second year of the marriage a daughter was born to them – an only child as it happened. Edward made a portmanteau of his wife's Christian names Caroline Alice, and created the name 'Carice' with which the child was christened. She was a beautiful little girl but sad, for from the time she could understand anything she was charged to keep silence lest she disturb her father's immortal concentration. In each of their houses Carice was given a room well away from the study and living rooms, and often in the servants' quarters. She was left in charge of maids, housekeepers, and friends when her parents went abroad for their holidays, and at the earliest possible moment she was sent as a boarder to school – even though the school was less than a mile from her parents' home. She was discouraged from pursuing a real interest in music for fear of the sounds of her childish practising.

Edward Elgar and his daughter Carice (1890–1970), *c.* 1900.

Yet in my own friendship with Carice, I found her the soul of loyalty and generous, intelligent help. Her father appreciated some of Carice's sterling qualities, and half acknowledged them. But as she was his own flesh, he could never quite believe in her without the aid of Alice: and that was the one aid Alice sometimes denied. Edward Elgar's nieces and nephews, the children of his sister Pollie, had far more of his unabashed affection than his daughter: but then Pollie's children always had more real affection in their own home. Edward and Alice were anything but ideal parents – two brainy people absorbed in each other, their relations with the outside world haunted by many spectres. Asked years later about her experience of family life with a genius, Carice responded: 'I wouldn't say it was always easy. After all, being the only child, I was somewhat sacrificed to the moods and needs of the moment.'

Dominated by her parents, she found it hard in later life to make level relationships of her own. At the age of 31 she married a man several years her senior, a Sussex sheep farmer with whom she had little in common: there were no children. Carice never rebelled, and as a result she kept many of her parents' best qualities, and none of their worst. But she lacked their creative talent.

In later life, when Alice was dead and Carice married and away, Elgar surrounded himself with family surrogates. He moved from London back to Worcestershire, partly to be near his sister Pollie and her loving family. Her daughters were constant visitors to the houses of his late years, and one or other often acted as their uncle's hostess for considerable periods. In addition he gathered a little staff. The elegant Mary Clifford, niece of the Elgars' housekeeper in London but highly literate and sophisticated, became his secretary. The rest were Worcestershire people – Richard Mountford, who went everywhere with him as valet and chauffeur, Dick's wife Fanny as cook, Fanny's sister Nellie as parlourmaid. Then there were his beloved dogs (who will have a section to themselves in Chapter 7).

Edward Elgar, then, was a family man extraordinarily dependent on those around him who enjoyed greater self-possession than he could find in himself. The return he made for their love and self-sacrifice was not directly to themselves, but to their world and ours. Their achievement lay in their understanding acceptance. Without them Edward Elgar would never have become the subject for such a book as this.

2

Creative Friendships

S OME THEMES GO with my friends: in my mind this goes with you: but if *feels*
artistic & striving, *educated* (!) and *courteous* only to a limited degree: you are
'more than all that' & my dear friend.

So Elgar wrote when sending a fragment of his oratorio *The Kingdom* to
Ivor Atkins in 1906.

Elgar's insecurity made his friendships both vital and varied. His
male friendships tended to run along the lines of the interest in music
shared with his father. His friendships with women pursued the
personal goals embodied in the influence of his mother. What was
uncommon about Elgar's friendships among both sexes was his use of
the friendships themselves for creative purposes. This idiosyncracy led
him eventually to his most celebrated work, the *'Enigma' Variations*.

These friendships, as with many or even most in Elgar's life,
contributed as much to his work as to his personal happiness. But that
distinction applies less to a creative artist than to almost anyone else.
Every person who has ever befriended an artist must at one time or
another expect to be used in ways which might be unacceptable in
ordinary friendship. Elgar's magnetism was such that he found devoted
and valuable friends at every stage of his career eager to do everything
they could for him.

Friends of Early Years

His first friend, and one to be entwined with music all his life, was
Hubert Leicester (1855–1939). He was the nephew of the man who had
persuaded W. H. Elgar to take the organist's job at the Catholic Church,
and son of the man who persuaded the elder Elgar to open the music
shop a few doors away from the Leicester printing shop in the Worcester
High Street. Hubert filled the role of elder brother for Edward after the
death of Harry Elgar in 1864. He was first charged with showing

Edward the way to school (which involved crossing the River Severn by ferry), and a lifelong friendship began. Together they explored the old city in which they lived, and of which Hubert one day would become Mayor. They rang the bells at St. Helen's Parish Church across the High Street from the family shops, before rushing off to mass at the Catholic Church where Hubert sang in the choir and Edward often played the organ. After the retirement of W. H. Elgar, Edward took over the organistship for two years, while Hubert became choirmaster and – typically – held the post for the rest of his life, a span of half a century. While Edward travelled far in life, Hubert remained at home, gaining a knighthood in the last year of his life for his services to 'the Faithful City' of Worcester.

Elgar (in Yale University doctoral robes) and Hubert Leicester emerging from the Worcester Guildhall, 12 September 1905. Leicester, as Mayor, has just presented his boyhood friend with the Freedom of the City.

When Edward visited Worcester in later years, he often stayed with Hubert and his family, where he found the warmth of ordinary family happiness often missing from his own haunted existence. Hubert's eldest son Philip recalled Edward saying his life gave him little happiness, whereupon Hubert replied that he himself was the happiest man in the city. Yet Philip's wife, whom I knew well over many years, recalled often the lasting pleasure each took in the other's company – Edward's eyes sparkling as he rattled out some familiar reminiscence or foolery, Hubert basking in the warmth of matchless companionship. When in 1907–8 Edward revived the sketches for his childhood family play music as *The Wand of Youth*, he dedicated the second Suite to Hubert. In 1930, when Hubert published a book on *Forgotten Worcester*, Edward contributed a Foreword to recall the sun shining golden over their shared schooldays: 'In our old age, with our undimmed affection, the sun still seems to show us a golden "beyond".'

If the first of Elgar's male friendships was cloudless and lifelong, his first close relation with a girl presaged a life of constant attraction and some trouble. Helen Weaver, the daughter of a shoe merchant in the Worcester High Street, became Edward's ideal when both were in their early twenties. Helen was intelligent and musical. Her family sent her to study in Leipzig, which was every music student's dream then. Edward had pleaded with his own parents to let him go, but as they could not afford such an education for all of their children the chance was denied to Edward. In the winter of 1882–83, when he was 25, he scraped together enough money for a New Year visit of three weeks to Leipzig. There he took full advantage of the concerts and opera performances, always in Helen's company. When Helen returned to Worcester for the summer of 1883, he persuaded her to an engagement. But the illness and death of her mother that autumn seemed to focus so many doubts that early the next year she broke the engagement. Young Elgar was heartbroken, as he wrote to a friend who was himself about to marry: ' . . . Accept my good wishes for your happiness, these I can give you the more sincerely since I know what it is to have lost my own forever.' Subsequent events were to suggest that this evaluation was not so far from the mark. In later life Elgar seems to have discussed Helen Weaver with nobody; she remains to this day a shadowy figure.

Elgar's creative talent began to be recognised in the environs of Worcester around 1880. E. W. Whinfield, a prosperous organ builder, held regular musical evenings at Severn Grange, his large house north of Worcester. Whinfield was pleased indeed to welcome the young Elgar, lending him books from his library in exchange for advice in arranging this or that score for the ensemble of accomplished amateur musicians who came for musical evenings.

The pianist of those evenings was one of the most able musicians in the district. Mrs. Harriet Fitton (1834–1924) had studied with a pupil of Chopin, and might have made a concert career had she not preferred the life of a married woman and mother of a large family. Young Elgar began visiting their house in Malvern for sessions of chamber music which included Beethoven, Mendelssohn, Schumann, and Brahms.

Before her own children were ready to participate, Mrs. Fitton used to secure another young man from outside the family to take the cello part in trios. One of these cellists was Henry Bellasis, a pupil of Cardinal Newman's at the Birmingham Oratory, where both he and his elder brother Richard were priests. Fr. Richard Bellasis was to be of help with the literary negotiations over Elgar's setting of Newman's *The Dream of Gerontius* (1900), and partly because of his friendship Elgar gave his manuscript score of *Gerontius* to the Oratory, where it is still to be seen. Mrs. Fitton's other cellist was a young Anglican curate in one of the Worcester parishes, Edward Capel-Cure. In later years he became the librettist for Elgar's first oratorio *The Light of Life* (1896), and gave advice over Elgar's own compilation of his libretto for *The Apostles* (1903). But Capel-Cure was a rather fiery character, and Elgar ultimately looked elsewhere for theological counsel.

In the 1880s and 1890s – years before these events of his creative maturity – Elgar also went to the Fitton home to teach music to Mrs. Fitton's daughters. When the daughters grew up, the Fittons amongst themselves could put together an excellent piano quartet. The violist was the tall and beautiful daughter Isabel (1868–1936), for whom Elgar the teacher devised an exercise for crossing strings. But then, with his thoughts entirely on composition, he was anything but a good teacher. In the end Isabel stopped her lessons, and when he begged her to resume, she replied: 'No, dear Edward, I value our friendship far too much.'

Elgar's marriage in 1889 brought some trouble to his wife from former friends who cut her socially for marrying 'beneath' her. But those who did not cut Alice became Edward's friends as well. Chief among these were the Baker family. They lived comfortably in the Gloucestershire countryside on 'new' money made by an uncle in the Midlands. The brother, William (1857–1935) a peppery little man and very musical, did himself well with his big house Hasfield Court, membership in the local hunt, and all the appurtenances of the country gentry which Elgar until now had approached only in the role of music teacher. He liked 'Billy' Baker and his hospitable wife enormously, and found in the country house visits to Hasfield Court the beginnings of a life he had always dreamt of. One Baker sister, Dora, was married to R. B. Townshend, a character if ever there was one. His early adventures in the American west had produced two books, and his quirky energy equalled that of his brother-in-law. He taught Elgar golf – a useful acquisition for one proposing to move with the county gentry. When not at Hasfield, the Townshends had a house in Oxford, and there also the Elgars were made welcome.

But Alice Elgar's special friend was the other Baker sister, Mary

**Elgar boating on the lake at Hasfield Court,
September 1901.**

Frances (affectionately known as 'Minnie'). She also had a house at Hasfield, and was among the very first of Alice's friends to encourage the engagement and the marriage. She dubbed Elgar 'Sir' long before his knighthood in 1904. At her house he was able to relax so far as to call for champagne in a bedroom jug as he worked at the last scene of *The Black Knight* (1892), where the Knight drinks his toast: it was known to the friends ever afterwards as 'the Perrier Jouet theme'. The same summer Minnie Baker took the Elgars for their first visit to Bayreuth, and then for a week to the Bavarian Alps. The Wagner operas made an enormous impression – especially *Parsifal*, which in those days could be seen in staged production only at Bayreuth. The Bavarian experience led to further holidays there, which in 1895 culminated in a choral suite, *From the Bavarian Highlands*, with words by Alice and fresh, vital music by Edward.

Minnie Baker's spinsterhood lasted longer than Alice's, but in the early 1890s she married the rector of Wolverhampton, Alfred Penny, a widower. He was another delightful man, with the capacity of ready understanding. And when the Elgars first visited the Pennys in Wolverhampton in 1895, Alfred Penny's 21-year-old daughter Dora (1874–1964) was smitten with Mr. Elgar in a way that changed her life. He responded to this hero-worship with an affection which was encouraged by Alice, with her watchful benevolence. Several ladies were to have such strong feelings about him, and of these Dora Penny was perhaps the first.

She set herself to entertain the Elgars, and especially Mr. Elgar when she could get him to herself. She began to bicycle the forty miles and more to pay them weekend and week-long visits at their home, helping in the household with everything from shopping to pasting the rapidly accumulating news cuttings of his career into folio albums under Alice's direction. Recalling a Mozartean extract from the Worcester Glee Club repertoire of his youth, Elgar dubbed her 'My sweet Dorabella', and she felt the world was hers. But the role of unrestrained youth became more difficult to sustain as Dora lived through her thirties. At 40 she married at last, and began her family.

After an initial year in London following their marriage, the Elgars had returned to Malvern, where he could at least scrape a living as a teacher while trying to compose. They negotiated the lease of a modest house. The solicitor who advised them had a cousin, Basil Nevinson, a capable amateur cellist, who played chamber music with his pianist friend, Hew Steuart-Powell. Basil Nevinson was a London gentleman, whose big house in Chelsea soon became a *pied-à-terre* for the Elgars' London visits.

His brother had an architectural practice in Malvern, where the assistant was Arthur Troyte Griffith, a retiring young bachelor whose thin height and wispy moustache were often said to give him a resemblance to Robert Louis Stevenson. Elgar had another nickname for him, based on his figure – 'the Ninepin'. Troyte Griffith was no musician himself, and he proved that when Elgar tried to teach him the rudiments of the piano. Yet he was so passionately fond of music, or perhaps of the idea of music, that he became one of its moving forces in Malvern. He founded a Concert Club to bring the great performers of the day to the town. His friendship for Elgar amounted almost to hero-worship. But tact and intelligence served him equally well, and very quickly Elgar came to rely on his intimate friendship – a friendship as complete as that with Hubert Leicester. In each case the friend's role as acolyte opened the way to an intimacy especially treasured by Elgar.

Cathedral organists

The same sort of friendship was offered by the organists of the Three Choirs Cathedrals. At the home Cathedral of Worcester there was Hugh Blair, who in 1892 cajoled Elgar into finishing his first major choral work, *The Black Knight*, after it had been on the stocks for three years, and then set about organising the first performance and ensuring its success. Three years later Blair bullied Elgar into realising his first big abstract work in a four-movement Organ Sonata, of which Blair gave the premiere in Worcester Cathedral. The premiere was not a success, because Elgar had taken so long to complete the Sonata that Blair had only four days in which to study a very rough manuscript for a work of virtuoso difficulty. The Sonata has posed a profound musical challenge to organists ever since. In 1897 Blair departed from the Cathedral under a cloud: drink was said to be at the bottom of it, but Cathedral politics resembled the world of Trollope novels, and who could say what the real causes were? However it happened, Worcester lost an enthusiastic and energetic musician, who thereafter pursued his career in London and retained Elgar's friendship to the end of his life.

Blair's successor at Worcester was Ivor Atkins (1867–1953), whose tenure of the Cathedral organistship lasted an astonishing fifty-three years until 1950 – many years after Elgar's death. Here was another of the great friendships of Elgar's life. Through a long and affectionate correspondence, Elgar nicknamed Atkins 'Firapeel' after the leopard in *Reynart the Foxe*. Elgar himself was Reynart, and that defined the relationship. Atkins asked Elgar to be godfather to his only son (who is now chairman of the trustees responsible for the keeping of the birthplace cottage at Broadheath, which Elgar himself wished preserved as his memorial).

At Gloucester for much of Elgar's career was Alfred Herbert Brewer (1865–1928), a man of immense energy, musical vision (often at loggerheads with a really remarkable series of reactionary Bishops and Deans), and considerable talent as a composer. The spectacle of the immense contralto Clara Butt singing Brewer's *The Fairy Pipers* must have been one of the best experiences of an era rich in such nonsense.

Elgar's affection for Brewer emerged most memorably in 1901: discovering that Brewer was about to withdraw his own oratorio *Emmaus* from the Gloucester Festival programme because he lacked the time to score it, Elgar took over Brewer's vocal score and orchestrated the work for his friend in ten days, thus saving the performance and probably the work. Brewer's musical sympathies sometimes went beyond Elgar's own: when he succeeded in introducing a work of Scriabin to a Cathedral programme, Elgar made it known that he thought things had gone too far. Yet the tables were sometimes turned. Brewer's son Charles (who was to have a distinguished career in the B.B.C.) told me of a Festival when Elgar was visiting, and Brewer senior solemnly warned his son against playing any music-hall tunes during the week. What was the father's astonishment when soon the latest 'hit' came crashing out of Charles's piano behind closed doors. The enraged man tore up the stairs and flung open the door – to find Charles and Elgar seated side by side thundering out the new tune for all to hear within Cathedral earshot.

During preparations for the 1928 Gloucester Festival Brewer suddenly died. He was succeeded by his pupil Herbert Sumsion, who had the immense task of rehearsing all the programmes and being chief conductor at his first Festival. Elgar was fond of the young man, and at the end of the successful Festival perpetrated a pun: 'What at the beginning of the week was As*sumption* is now Certainty.'

At Hereford was Atkins's teacher, G. R. Sinclair (1863-1917). A crusty bachelor, Sinclair shared his house in the Hereford Cathedral Close with a large bulldog, Dan. When Elgar came to visit, he often wrote in Sinclair's Visitors' Book musical fragments illustrating 'The Moods of Dan' – 'he muses (on the muzzling order)', 'triumphant (after a fight)', and so on. One of these became the 'Prayer' motive in *Gerontius*; another was to become the primary subject of the Overture *In The South* (1904). Sinclair was a real eccentric who, despite being the younger, set himself up as a kind of uncle-figure in Elgar's early days as a composer.

When Sinclair died suddenly in 1917, the Hereford organistship was held open for his favourite pupil and assistant, Percy Clark Hull, until he could take it up at the end of the First World War. 'P.C.', as his friends always knew him, could never forget that Elgar had dedicated *Pomp and Circumstance* Marches to Sinclair and Atkins, and was determined to have one for himself. His badgering resulted in *Pomp and Circumstance No. 5*, dedicated to P. C. Hull, in 1930. It was the first sign of Elgar's return to serious composition after his wife's death ten years earlier, and it remains in my view the finest of his short marches.

Encouragers

Through Elgar's years in Malvern (1891–1904), he was also befriended by several women. The most interesting of these was Rosa Burley (1866–1951), the young headmistress of 'The Mount', one of the schools where for his sins Elgar taught the violin. Miss Burley had recently purchased the school, and was determined to put it on the map. She was

**Rosa Burley
in later life,
c. 1915.**

a woman of strong intellect and stronger emotions. Though she soon identified Elgar as 'one of the most difficult problems that faced me in the management of the school' because he was an inexpert teacher, she was so struck with his creative promise and problems that she set herself the task of trying to reconcile them. She enrolled herself as his private violin pupil; when she had progressed far enough she joined the amateur orchestras he conducted. She started an instrumental ensemble at her school partly for the purpose (as she herself admitted) of trying over music with which he wished to familiarise himself, despite the fact that much of it was of a difficulty far beyond them. At the school she made herself his artistic confidante, and there is no doubt that her keen and youthful intellect, genius for languages (she was to become an important member of the Government Censorship during the First World War), and ready sympathy made her a uniquely stimulating companion in the Malvern of the 1890s. She accompanied him on many long bicycle rides, though too often other young ladies of the school joined them. When the Elgars removed from Malvern in 1904 Miss Burley was so upset that she closed her school and went abroad for several years as a governess. Back in England when the Elgars moved to London in 1912, she established herself in Highgate across the Heath from their Hampstead home, to which she came very often. But when Lady Elgar died, Miss Burley's jealousy overcame her: she betrayed herself by suggesting to Elgar's daughter Carice that she had been more than Carice's schoolmistress. It put an instant end to the friendship, and Elgar never saw her again. Yet Rosa Burley was haunted all through her remaining years by her memories of Elgar's friendship, even as Dora Penny was. And like Dora Penny, Miss Burley made her memories into a book. It is a curious document, largely ghost-written and overweening in tone, yet with some of the sharpest insights into the characters of Elgar and his wife. It was Miss Burley who said of Alice: 'Hers was truly a great love.'

Another sophisticated woman in the Malvern area was Lady Mary Lygon (1869–1927), the younger sister of the Earl of Beauchamp at Madresfield. Lady Mary was a great patron of music in the district, and she founded the Madresfield Musical Competition. During the 1890s she knew Elgar mostly as an adjudicator at her festivals and through the Worcestershire Philharmonic Society, a choral and orchestral body founded in 1898 for him to conduct. Later, especially after Elgar's knighthood and his appearance in Court circles, the friendship became a warm one.

The Worcestershire Philharmonic Society had two secretaries. One was Isabel Fitton. The other was Winifred Norbury (1861–1938), one of a large family living in a big old house standing at the base of the Malvern Hills. Winifred and her sister Florence were of Elgar's own generation, but spiritually they lived a century in the past. From one end of their lives to the other – right up into the 1930s – they never set foot in a shop. Yet the Norburys were keen and intelligent admirers of Elgar's genius. Winifred was just the comfortable, witty sort of personality to broaden him while 'keeping him in order', as they used to express it.

Another friend associated with the Worcestershire Philharmonic and also with golf was Richard Arnold, a son of the poet Matthew Arnold. He was one of the first of the residents of Worcester to recognise the true extent of Elgar's genius. When Elgar played his sketches for *King Olaf* in 1895, Arnold's wife wrote to Alice:

It will give the world a chance of learning that there is great musical genius *yet* to be found – Dick has come home perfectly *possessed* by Mr. Elgar & his wonderful cleverness (that is hardly the word) – He says Schumann was a babe compared to him, & can think & talk of *nothing* else . . .

That cleverness, or talent, or genius was beginning to attract the attention of others farther afield. In 1897, after several years of relations with the leading publisher of choral music in London, Novello, one employee recognised Elgar's pre-eminence among all the composers on the firm's books. The employee's views were the more interesting because he himself was German. August Johannes Jaeger, born in Düsseldorf in 1860, became the first encourager in a professional position to convince Elgar of his own worth, and to persuade him to pursue and realise his dreams.

It was the greatest service that anyone outside his immediate family could do for Elgar. As he came to the fore in provincial choral festivals with more and more distinctive and imposing works, audiences exposed to his music began to acknowledge its power. But for the self-taught composer, every success raised the standard by which any new work must be judged, and courage was often overcome by despair. In later years Elgar found many friends to talk him out of his fears. But of all those far from home, the first was A. J. Jaeger, the small German whose enthusiasm was for the fortunes of music in his adopted land.

Through the decade that remained before Jaeger's early death in 1909, he cajoled, persuaded, and occasionally blackmailed Elgar into writing, and especially rewriting, his music until it was better than the composer himself might have dreamed. One extraordinary example of this persuasion was the climax in *The Dream of Gerontius*. Elgar felt that the climax came with the great chorus of Angelicals, 'Praise to the Holiest', by no means at the end of the work; the remainder, dealing with the Soul's going before God prior to its journey to Purgatory, must be all anticlimax. Jaeger passionately disagreed, saying that the real climax had to be the Soul's sight of God. Elgar protested with Catholic theology, saying that though the Soul goes into God's presence, the audience must be kept outside. Jaeger retorted that Wagner, even in *Parsifal*, never preferred theology before musical drama; and by rating Elgar 'no Wagner' at last brought him round. The climax as finally realised (precisely according to Jaeger's suggestions) is one of the chief reasons for the general opinion ranking *The Dream of Gerontius* as Elgar's greatest work.

Jaeger, in addition to the loving admiration offered by all of Elgar's friends, brought to this friendship a quality rare indeed: the ability to show his friend how to make his expression more powerful than Elgar would have done left to his own devices. The other aspect of such a friendship was of course Elgar's own ability to recognise the value of this friend's advice over something so close to himself as the climax of a work of personal, private definition. It is a rare spirit who has the humility and courage for that.

'Enigma' Variations

Such were the friends in Elgar's mind one evening in October 1898, when he came home tired and depressed from a day's teaching at Miss Burley's school. A fortnight earlier he had conducted the premiere of his first major work to be produced at a festival of national consequence. The event was the Leeds Festival, and the work was the cantata *Caractacus*. His music had been welcomed at Leeds, but Elgar was dissatisfied. What he had really wanted to write was a symphony – a totally abstract work organised entirely in terms of his music and its needs without reference to any plot. Except for the *Froissart* Overture of 1890 and the Organ Sonata of 1895, all his attempts to write such a work had ended in failure – perhaps because self-teaching had not even yet, at the age of 41, given him the necessary experience. Now he had returned to the humdrum life of a local music teacher.

After dinner that evening he sat at the piano extemporising – disconsolately allowing his fingers to move over the keys without aim or purpose. Suddenly Alice, who was sitting by, exclaimed: 'Edward, that's a good tune!' He replied: 'Eh, tune? What tune?' He felt his way back to it – an entity which would never have been singled out from the texture of his wandering musical thoughts but for his wife's remark.

It became the 'Enigma' theme of the *Variations* which followed. Later speculation – some of it from people closely concerned who might have known better – insisted that this music must conceal some hidden musical polyphony or cipher. Elgar did say that there was a hidden 'theme' in the music. But he never said it was a tune. In view of the way the music started – by Alice's identification of something her husband would not have recognised as an entity – it seems clear that there could have been no deliberate musical concealment at the moment of invention: Elgar said specifically that the way he played the music that evening was 'as it now stands'. Moreover the variations which followed set about solving the 'Enigma' purely in terms of the original musical elements, without any revelation of a secret tune. The variations were Elgar's means of solving his Enigma. And these means have caught the imagination of audiences ever since.

When he was interrupted by his wife and then found his way back to the music she had noticed, Alice exclaimed: 'That's the tune! What is it?' He replied: 'Nothing. But something might be made of it.' Then, instead of thinking (as almost anyone else might have done) 'I will do so-and-so with it,' Elgar's mind went instead to his friends, his reassuring companions. Was it possible to 'look at' the strange tune through another's eyes, play it with some reference to a characteristic or an experience shared with that person? It was not an entirely new idea. Schumann had ciphered the initials of friends into his themes, and Chopin often amused his circle by extemporising a sketch of some trait or foible of a friend which all those present could instantly recognise.

August Johannes Jaeger

Elgar may have known of these precedents: but his action from this moment forward gave every indication of true spontaneity.

Possibly because Elgar was at this moment playing the piano, his mind went first to a pianist who had a recognisable characteristic. He thought of Hew Steuart-Powell, the pianist of his informal trio with Basil Nevinson. Steuart-Powell's habit was to run over the keys in a toccata-like exercise to warm up before a chamber music session. Elgar said to Alice: 'Powell would have done this:' and he twisted the 'Enigma' theme to a reminiscence of Steuart-Powell's piano run.

From there Elgar's mind went not to another pianist, but typically to the other instrument of the ensemble, Basil Nevinson's cello: 'Nevinson would have looked at it like this'. The music he played extended the tune in a tenor range evocation of cello *cantilena*. The remembrance of Nevinson gave Elgar's musical thoughts a new dimension, as he wrote afterwards:

The variation is a tribute to a very dear friend whose scientific and artistic attainments, and the whole-hearted way they were placed at the disposal of his friends, particularly endeared him to [me].

There it was then: an ensemble of friends, whose sequence of voices might give assurance and direction to the man whose creative desires still outran his self-assurance.

He turned to Alice again, with the thought of using the theme she had identified to show one of their friends so clearly that she might guess the identity from the music alone. He played the tune as a loud *Allegro di molto* with a humorous canon in the middle and a slam at the end, asking: 'Who is that like?' Alice hesitated for only an instant before responding: 'It is exactly the way Billy Baker goes out of the room.'

Other variations quickly followed. One suggested Alice herself, by letting into the 'Enigma' theme a little triplet figure he used to whistle by way of greeting to let her know he had come into the house. There was a skit on Billy Baker's brother-in-law Richard Townshend – another on Dora Penny, with her stammer incorporated in the middle of the theme – one to show the alternating seriousness and characteristic laugh of Richard Arnold – Isabel Fitton practising her viola exercise and then stepping lightly aside from her instruction – a tearing, roaring variation for Troyte Griffith, the most impetuous of men: this could play on his 'Ninepin' nickname, touch on his 'maladroit' attempts at the piano, or it might refer to a walk taken by the two of them that weekend on the Malverns in a thunderstorm. They ran for it, and sheltered at the Norburys' old house, Sherridge: and thereby another variation, first labelled '2 secretaries' of the Worcestershire Philharmonic, was fixed on Winifred Norbury. A big and serious *Adagio* variation recalled one of many encouraging private talks in which Jaeger compared Elgar with Beethoven: and the astounding thing was that the 'Enigma' tune was malleable enough not only to recall the notes of the 'Pathétique' Sonata

**The opening theme of the *'Enigma'* Variations.
Elgar's manuscript full score, 1899.**

slow movement, but to take on the nobility of a Beethoven *Adagio* as well.

The next weekend Elgar went to Hereford to visit the organist G. R. Sinclair. The two friends walked along the Wye with the bulldog Dan – who wandered too close to the steep bank, rolled down into the river, had to swim for it, and came out down below with a bark. 'Set that to music,' challenged Sinclair, thinking of the 'Moods of Dan' in his Visitors' Book. Elgar did, with the 'Enigma' tune once again as a basis, and so it became another variation.

Elgar with G. R. Sinclair (*lower left*) and the bulldog Dan, the violinist Max Mossel and Percy Hull (*top right*) in Sinclair's garden, Hereford Cathedral Close, 1896.

He projected several variations based on one or another professional musician – Sir Arthur Sullivan, Sir Hubert Parry, Ivor Atkins. But professional musicians made a dangerous basis for these variations, as their own musical characteristics kept obtruding on what was to be after all original music. Ultimately Elgar cast out all the portraits of professional musicians, leaving only amateurs, on whom his own tune could be easily imposed.

One of the variations began as Lady Mary Lygon. Lady Mary was soon to go far away, accompanying her brother to a colonial governorship in Australia. The 'Enigma' tune twisted to a familiar quotation from Mendelssohn's Overture *Calm Sea and Prosperous Voyage*. But with that the atmosphere of this variation turned far too portentous to suggest his almost casual acquaintance with the beautiful Lady Mary: the character of this music with her name attached would be certain to set local tongues wagging. So Elgar dedicated to Lady Mary a much lighter work, and turned the *Calm Sea* variation to a *Romanza* with three asterisks replacing any name or initials.

The *Calm Sea* variation was a late development, for these Variations had 'commenced' (as Elgar later wrote) 'in a spirit of humour & continued in deep seriousness'. The 'friends pictured within' the *Variations* had indeed given his music a new direction. Their 'views' of his tune made a collection of gestures and traits which he himself had noticed and which had appealed to him: and so their collection suggested a culmination in some final portrait of their composer. Thus Elgar's music could re-enact the process by which an unformed mind notices and imitates one idea from here, another from there, until an individuality is built up.

But what was the individuality of the composer's self-portrait? It was not to be 'E.E.' as he was. Rather he called it 'E.D.U.', referring to the diminutive of the German 'Eduard' by which Alice called him. So the final portrait would show not the man as he was, but his wife's vision of him – the vision which had identified the 'Enigma' theme and made what was to be its first variation, 'C.A.E.' This final variation began in assurance, almost swagger, and moved on to present the two phases of the 'Enigma' theme simultaneously, as mutual counterpoint. They did not quite fit together rhythmically. So the music recalled the whistle for Alice, and in came the music of her variation, to restore confidence and round out the whole experience in a cycle. 'E.D.U.' showed a man dependent on his friends, and most of all on his wife.

In this form the *'Enigma' Variations* were publicly performed twice before Jaeger persuaded Elgar to give 'E.D.U.' a more convincing end. (It was almost exactly the pattern of Jaeger's argument over *Gerontius* a year later.) Elgar declined, protested, and finally gave way – to produce the coda we know today, where the two parts of the theme are combined not simultaneously but one after the other to make a new, longer and more powerful melodic figure. This was a portent for Elgar's music in many ways. Never before or since has a great composer been so well served by his friends. Audience recognition of the score's warm-hearted generosity has played a major role in the music's popularity ever since.

The coda finally uniting the two 'Enigma' figures, 1899.

Friends of the Music

The man who conducted the *Variations* premiere was to occupy another important place in Elgar's friendship. He was the great German-Hungarian conductor Hans Richter (1843–1916). In that era of rivalry between the disciples of Wagner and Brahms, Richter was the disciple of both. The Richter Concerts, which Elgar had attended whenever he could get to London as a young man, played an important part in introducing Englishmen of Elgar's generation to Wagner. But Richter served Brahms as well. On one early occasion, when Elgar was in London for the first performance there of a small work of his own in the afternoon, he went in the evening to hear Richter conduct the English premiere of Brahms's Third Symphony. Ever afterwards this Symphony held a special place in Elgar's affection, and in later years when he conducted tours and concerts with the London Symphony Orchestra, his programmes included the Brahms Third again and again. Its use of a unifying 'motto' theme may well have given a hint for Elgar's First Symphony (1908).

As for Richter himself, Elgar was overjoyed at his acceptance of the *'Enigma' Variations* for performance in the Richter Concerts of 1899. Richter at once recognised Elgar's superiority over every other English composer of the day, and warm friendship soon followed. It was Richter's advocacy more than anything else that awakened the interest of continental Europe in Elgar, and led to repeated performances of his music by such great conductors as Arthur Nikisch and Fritz Steinbach. When Elgar was given a three-day Festival of his works at Covent Garden in 1904, it was Richter who conducted. Writing to the older man, Elgar began to subscribe himself 'Your godson', and once, 'Your son'. All this time Richter was endeavouring to persuade Elgar to write his Symphony, and Elgar promised Richter the dedication – if ever it was written. He had been collecting material for a work in Eb major (which ultimately became the Second Symphony), and in the autumn of 1905 wrote into his sketchbook an idea labelled 'Hans Himself!' as if it were another 'Enigma' Variation. It became the Finale second subject in the Eb Symphony of 1911. But it was the First Symphony of 1908 which he dedicated to Hans Richter – 'True artist & true friend'.

In addition to his concerts in London, Richter conducted the Birmingham Festivals and the Hallé Concerts in Manchester. This formed another tie with music in the north of England, and still others followed. In Liverpool the younger composer Granville Bantock (1868–1946) became a generous advocate and friend: again the friendship was to prove lifelong, and the closest of all Elgar's relations with the composers of his time. And Bantock introduced friends of his own.

One was the critic who called himself 'Ernest Newman' – an allegory indeed. Newman (1868–1959) had abilities that went far beyond ordinary musical criticism. He was unquestionably deeply devoted to Elgar, and was able to suggest again and again new directions for Elgar's art. Elgar responded with a trust and an intimacy he rarely conferred. It was Newman who urged him to get out of the oratorio field as soon as he could and devote himself to orchestral music. Elgar took several years to implement this advice, but when he did so the Symphonies and the Violin Concerto were the result. Then Newman played a role in persuading Elgar to abandon the Symphony for the symphonic poem or study on programmatic lines. The result was *Falstaff* (1913). *Falstaff* is still a controversial work, but there was no controversy about the composer's own estimate of it at the time as his finest work. Several years later, when Newman lost his wife, Elgar dedicated to him the valedictory Piano Quintet (1919).

Newman was one of the last people to see Elgar as he lay dying in 1934. Later the critic reported that Elgar had said five words to him which shed light on the man and his music, but which Newman refused to divulge. Here I think Newman's great veneration for Elgar betrayed him: if he did not intend to divulge the words, he ought to have kept the experience to himself. In any case, it is idle to suppose that a few words could significantly alter our understanding of a life whose whole study and success lay precisely in the ability to express itself. Elgar's music is sufficiently eloquent for any with ears to hear, as Newman would have been the first to agree. And as an experienced journalist, he ought to have known what the newspapers and public curiosity would do with such tantalisation as this offered. It is finally – almost alone of his critical utterances – of no importance.

Another Liverpool friend of Bantock's, and Newman's as well, was Alfred Rodewald (1861–1903), a businessman whose passion was music. Rodewald was Hans Richter's only conducting pupil, and he founded a fine amateur orchestra in Liverpool. Elgar dedicated *Pomp and Circumstance No. 1* to them and their conductor, Rodewald. He was a big man in every way. His qualities of genial strength and gentleness raised him high in Elgar's esteem and love. Rodewald's sudden death from influenza in November 1903 removed the first close friend of Elgar's own generation and shadowed his life for years afterward.

Two others were added to the list of Elgar's northern friends in his middle years. One was Nicholas Kilburn (1843–1923), a manufacturer and talented choral conductor at Bishop Auckland, Co. Durham. Kilburn's whole-hearted support of Elgar through friendship and performance and counsel won him the dedication of *The Music Makers* (1912). The other was Henry Embleton, a mining engineer who was secretary, treasurer, and patron of the Leeds Choral Union. Embleton was a wealthy man, but he virtually bankrupted himself in supporting choral tours, concerts, and performances of Elgar's music. It was Embleton who came as close as anyone to persuading Elgar that he could finish *The Apostles* trilogy. Embleton always evinced the kind of uncritical admiration which the emotional Elgar needed, but of which the creative Elgar could make little use. Kilburn, in his stiff, Old Testament prophetical way, did better to help by admiration mixed with counsel.

Friends in London had begun to gather round Elgar by the turn of the century. They came rapidly in the wake of the *'Enigma' Variations* success in 1899. Amongst the first were two families of Speyers who were cousins. Edward Speyer (1839–1934) was the son of a minor German composer whose household had welcomed Mendelssohn, Spohr, and almost every later German composer of distinction. His wife, a singing pupil of Julius Stockhausen, had been a favourite singer of Brahms. The Speyers welcomed Elgar at Ridgehurst, their big house in Hertfordshire, and eagerly enrolled him on their roster of Great Composers of Personal Acquaintance. He responded to their flattering affection, and to the splendid country house weekends which included such attractions as private performances by the Joachim Quartet. But ultimately, there was not the intellectual stimulation about his hosts to hold his interest. A typical picture is that of Speyer trying vainly to persuade Sir Edward to discourse on music, while the composer's fascination was glued to the Ridgehurst billiard table.

The other Speyer was Sir Edgar, a distinguished financier who headed the Queen's Hall Syndicate. His wife was the beautiful and accomplished Leonora von Stosch, a violin pupil of Ysaÿe who helped Elgar by trying over early drafts of the Violin Concerto. Sir Edgar conducted the negotiations which secured the completion of the Second Symphony for its premiere at Queen's Hall in 1911. In later years this Speyer was Elgar's trusted financial adviser, though he never secured him the opulence of which Elgar dreamed.

A much closer London friend was Leo Frank Schuster (1852–1927), the descendant of another powerful German banking family. Frank Schuster was unmarried, like his tall and elegant sister Adela. He devoted his best energies to the cultivation of music and musicians, both at his London house in Old Queen Street overlooking St. James's Park, and in a comfortable Thames-side house at Maidenhead. It was typical of his sensitivity to be hurt by a gentle Max Beerbohm caricature entitled 'Frank Schuster discovering a new pianist'.

He was a loyal friend to Elgar, and left no stone unturned to introduce him and his music to those whose influence counted. Schuster was indirectly responsible for the planned production of Elgar's *Coronation Ode* at Covent Garden in 1902, and for the introduction to King Edward VII and Queen Alexandra which followed. Schuster then made himself financially responsible for the three-day festival of Elgar's works at Covent Garden in March 1904, which led directly to Elgar's knighthood. Elgar dedicated to Schuster the Overture *In The South* which was produced at that Festival. The dedicatee received it as the greatest honour of his life.

ROYAL **OPERA,**

COVENT GARDEN.

Proprietors: THE GRAND OPERA SYNDICATE, Ltd.
Secretary & Business Manager: Mr. NEIL FORSYTH.

ELGAR FESTIVAL.

The Grand Opera Syndicate, by arrangement with Mr. Alfred Schulz-Curtius,
will hold a

MUSICAL FESTIVAL

consisting of the principal Works of

Dr. EDWARD ELGAR

AT

THE ROYAL OPERA, COVENT GARDEN,

ON

MONDAY, MARCH 14th, at 8 p.m.
TUESDAY, MARCH 15th, at 8 p.m.
WEDNESDAY, MARCH 16th, at 8 p.m.

The Works will be produced under the direction of

Dr. HANS RICHTER

and rendered by the

HALLÉ ORCHESTRA OF 100 PERFORMERS,

THE MANCHESTER CHORUS OF 275 VOICES,

And the following Distinguished Soloists
(Arranged alphabetically):

Mesdames: CLARA BUTT,	Messieurs: ANDREW BLACK,
KIRKBY LUNN,	JOHN COATES,
AGNES NICHOLLS.	D. FFRANGCON-DAVIES,
	KENNERLEY RUMFORD.

Dr. Hans Richter having, with his Manchester Orchestra and Chorus, devoted
special attention to Dr. Elgar's Works, a perfect ensemble may be anticipated.

FOR FURTHER PARTICULARS PLEASE TURN OVER.

Prospectus for the Elgar Festival, March 1904.

Through the years Schuster gave Elgar elaborate gifts, hospitality, and unashamed love. After a performance of *Gerontius* in 1903 Schuster wrote:

In the matter of friendship we are, and I thank God for it, on terms of equality, but try as I may, I can never forget that *you* have written a 'Gerontius' and *I* have only listened to it! – the gap *awes* me.

Stated that way it could awe Elgar himself, and it did not always help when Frankie quoted Walt Whitman on the nature of comradeship. Elgar was sometimes impatient. But it was hard to resist the tribute of a private seventieth birthday concert in 1927 organised by Schuster partly to introduce Elgar's chamber music to a new generation of listeners including William Walton, Constant Lambert, the Sitwells, and Siegfried Sassoon. At the end of that year Schuster died, and left Elgar £7000 because he 'saved my country from the reproach of having produced no composer worthy to rank with the Great Masters'. After Frank's death Elgar maintained a courtly and affectionate relationship with his elder sister Adela, a lady of fine intellect and gentle spirit.

Among Schuster's closest friends were the Member of Parliament for Sheffield, Charles Stuart-Wortley, and his wife Alice (a daughter of the painter Millais). Here began one of the great friendships of Elgar's life, and to understand it we must remember that every male–female relationship in those days was not necessarily seen as implying sexual liaison. The Elgars and the Stuart-Wortleys carried on a four-cornered friendship that went from each to all and all to each throughout their lives. Charles Stuart-Wortley was a cultured and sophisticated man, a fine amateur musician who would habitually soothe the rigours of a day in Parliament with an hour's accomplished playing from Wagner vocal scores at the piano in his big house in Cheyne Walk, Chelsea. He was so touched by the first version of the Violin Concerto slow movement when he heard Elgar try it over with Lady Speyer that he begged for the loan of the manuscript to play it for himself. Elgar made his friend a present of the manuscript: at that moment the fate of the Concerto hung in the balance, and Stuart-Wortley's manful and tactful encouragement was almost certainly a factor in the work's successful completion.

The Concerto's real muse, however, was Alice Stuart-Wortley. The friendship had grown slowly from 1902, and all of the people directly involved realised and quietly assented to the composer's need to project himself and his work at that moment upon Alice Stuart-Wortley. The dignity with which this was managed, and the increase of love and friendship which came out of it for all concerned, may stand as a tribute to the people and their time. All were by 1910 well known in London circles. Today the rapacity of the media for sensation in high places would make such delicacy virtually impossible.

For Elgar, two of the themes of his evolving Concerto were associated with the windflower (*Anemone nemorosa*) of early spring in his home

Elgar and W. H. Reed, Gloucester 1922.

countryside. This little flower he associated in turn with Alice Stuart-Wortley. Throughout the composition of the Concerto in the first half of 1910 her presence was demanded and secured again and again – sometimes the two of them alone, often with his own Alice welcomed and welcoming, and occasionally (when his busy life permitted) with Stuart-Wortley himself smiling on the evolution of a masterpiece through his wife's powers of sympathy, tact, and friendship. It was a further extension of the *'Enigma' Variations* principle in Elgar's music.

Friends in the Profession

All of these London friends were amateurs of music, like the *Variations* subjects. In London and elsewhere Elgar acquired a vast acquaintanceship amongst professional musicians, especially after the turn of the century, when every orchestra and choral society in the land and many abroad were eager to be conducted by him. *Cockaigne* (1900–1) was dedicated 'to my many friends, the members of British orchestras', and it was no idle gesture. Sometimes a favourite soloist, like the contralto Muriel Foster or David Ffrangçon-Davies, became something more than a professional friend.

Yet perhaps it is significant that Elgar's closest friend amongst professional musicians was a man noticeably younger in years and smaller in stature. He was William Henry Reed (1876–1942), a violinist in the London Symphony Orchestra. The intimacy began when Elgar felt he needed someone other than Lady Speyer to help him with the Violin Concerto – perhaps a masculine player. He had known Reed for several years before the day in 1910 when he suddenly came up to him and asked for his help. The younger man was thunderstruck, yet the friendship ripened from that moment with extraordinary speed. The day of Elgar's approach to Reed, almost precisely the first anniversary of Jaeger's death, leads to the speculation that Reed may have been chosen as a possible replacement to Jaeger, whom he closely resembled.

Cast unmistakably in the role of counsellor, Reed was never openly critical, as Jaeger sometimes had been: Reed's youth and innate modesty precluded that. But he was keenly intelligent and observant – qualities which later produced two books that are amongst the most valuable ever written about Elgar. During the twenty years and more of their intimacy, Reed could often make a suggestion with humour that was irresistible. Yet he was keenly responsive to Elgar's moods, having a God-given quality of sympathetic silence when it was needed. Altogether it is fair to say that Reed became the closest friend of Elgar's later life; and the friendship tells a great deal about Elgar. Amongst all the composers, conductors, writers, and statesmen he knew, he chose this small, intelligent man of humour and consummate tact, a perfect embodiment of the worthwhile companion who would never threaten him.

Toward the end of his life Elgar added to the friendship with Reed another with a man in many ways similar, the recording manager Fred Gaisberg (1873–1951). Gaisberg could be decisive and cutting when his profession called for it; yet his long and intimate correspondence with Elgar shows him as another of the rare spirits who could help Elgar by giving the most practical encouragement. The intimacy with Gaisberg blossomed with the advent of microphone recording in 1925. In the remaining years of Elgar's life, Gaisberg saw to it that he conducted recordings of virtually all of his major orchestral works. Elgar became the first composer to be so well served by the gramophone. Gaisberg recognised Elgar's abilities as a conductor to convey the spirit of his own music, and saw that for Elgar more than for most composers the shaping of the performance was a final step in the creative process.

There can be no doubt that the existence of Elgar's recorded interpretations has been of benefit, especially to conductors coming to his music for the first time: Sir Georg Solti has put on record his own indebtedness to Elgar's recordings. Beyond that, the Elgar interpretations are of such quality that their preservation may well have the effect of aiding the reputation of the music itself for posterity. That again would represent a first in musical history, but by no means a last. Elgar was fascinated with inventions. But he was also deeply mistrustful of the future. His long and unbroken love-affair with the gramophone was pre-eminently the achievement of Gaisberg – who worked through modesty and tact and humour, much as Billy Reed worked through the same years. There was not a shadow of rivalry between the two, but warm friendship and understanding at every moment.

With English composers of his own time Elgar maintained largely wary relations. He acknowledged the friendly help of Sir Arthur Sullivan (1842–1900) and Sir Hubert Parry (1848–1918), and with the latter evolved a warm correspondence despite the fact that Parry was not an expert orchestrator, an accomplishment Elgar always rated very highly. (Elgar's friendship with Richard Strauss (1864–1949), fragmented by distance and war but never broken, rested largely on a mutual admiration of each other's abilities as orchestrators.) With Parry's colleague Sir Charles Stanford (1852–1924), the case was different. Stanford also tried to help Elgar, especially in the early days; but the brisk assurance with which Stanford pursued everything in life seemed to Elgar to border on cocksureness and patronage. They had a parting of the ways, occasioned probably by Stanford's rising jealousy of Elgar's influence, and by Elgar's outspoken criticisms of the English musical scene over which Stanford wielded such power. Much has been written of the rights and wrongs in this case of conflicting personalities. But one thing that did not help Stanford's case with Elgar was that for all his skill as a teacher Stanford wrote too much: his music seldom shows any stylistic individuality, and is (as Elgar once wrote to Jaeger) 'neither fish, flesh, fowl, nor good red-herring'. Stanford's influence in his day was out of all proportion to his creative importance, and Elgar could not stand that. Posterity has proved him right.

Among younger composers, perhaps Elgar's closest friend after Granville Bantock was the quiet Walford Davies (1869–1941). He was another composer who failed to find great creative individuality, but then he never made such a show of influence-wielding as Stanford had done. And being younger, and a man of real sympathy, he did not threaten the self-taught Elgar.

The English composer whose music Elgar loved best was Edward German (1862–1936), the composer of *Merrie England*, incidental music to *Henry VIII* and *Nell Gwyn*, and other stage successes of the day. He was another small and modest man, not easy to know. But he was Sullivan's disciple, and his melodic invention was as distinctive as Stanford's was grey. Elgar had a vein of intimate, light music in himself, as evidenced by such successes as *Salut d'amour* and *Chanson de matin*. Occasionally, as in the Piano Quintet, he tried to reconcile this easy vein of melody with a serious effort. He was practically the only composer of his generation to make the attempt.

With composers younger still Elgar's relations tended to be a little distant. He showed affection for Bantock's pupil Julius Harrison as a Worcestershire man. He befriended the struggling Havergal Brian and Josef Holbrooke, and invited him to conduct a work of his own in the London Symphony Orchestra concerts. But he could not manufacture a musical sympathy that was not there. He gave willing advice to John Ireland, and carried Gloucester Festival invitations for new works to Eugene Goossens and Arthur Bliss (whose musical rhodomontade

Gloucester Festival, 1922: (*left to right*) Arthur Bliss, Herbert Brewer, W. H. Reed, Elgar, Eugene Goossens.

**Elgar with his daughter Carice
and Fred Gaisberg (*right*),
in W. H. Reed's garden at
Croydon, 2 June 1933.
They are toasting Elgar's
76th birthday and a safe return
by air from France, where Elgar
and Gaisberg had visited Delius.**

repelled him). He was deeply impressed with only one composer of that
generation, Rutland Boughton (1878–1960). Moved by Boughton's
opera *The Immortal Hour*, as many listeners were, Elgar gave his name
to a movement to establish a festival of Boughton's works at
Glastonbury. But Boughton's talent, like Elgar's own, found its
wellsprings in the attitudes of the old world destroyed by the First
World War: there was little place for his kind of Celtic twilight in the
years following 1918. Boughton none the less remained deeply grateful
to Elgar to the end of his life, evincing a veneration for Elgar, his music,
and his vision in every word he spoke to me about him.

With Frederick Delius (1862–1934) Elgar began a late, courtly correspondence. As Master of the King's Music Elgar tried hard to get an honour for Delius and succeeded. When finally they met in 1933, the last full year of life for both of them, the success was personal rather than musical. Like most composers who really succeed in projecting themselves in their art, Elgar derived his deepest satisfaction from his own music. And feeling this, it was less easy to befriend other composers than to share his most private inspiration and spontaneity with admiring amateurs who had no creative visions of their own to oppose to his.

Private Friends of Later Life

Among the friends of Elgar's later life were several middle-aged or elderly women in addition to Adela Schuster. One was Mrs. Julia Worthington, a wealthy American hostess whose delightful companionship promptly overcame a prejudice against Americans. Mrs.Worthington's friendship meant so much that Dora Penny thought she might have been a secret dedicatee of the Violin Concerto. No independent evidence of this is known, but Mrs.Worthington's death in 1912 left both the Elgars disconsolate for months.

Mrs. Marie Joshua was German, a friend of Hans Richter's, born with a certainty (as her granddaughter described it to me) that music was a German monopoly. That was before Richter sent her to hear Elgar's First Symphony. She became an instant convert, and her enthusiasm thereafter was only matched by her motherly affection. Again the affection was for both the Elgars. Elgar dedicated the Violin Sonata, finished just as she died, to her memory.

Then there was Frances Colvin (the 'Madonna' of Robert Louis Stevenson) and her husband Sidney (1845–1927). Mrs. Colvin (1839–1924), like the others, fulfilled some aspects of a mother's role in the years after the death of Elgar's mother in 1902. Her husband was the friend of many poets and writers, and at one time negotiated between Elgar and Thomas Hardy for the production of an opera: to our cost, he was unsuccessful. Where Colvin did succeed was in bringing Elgar together with the poet whose work provided the finest verse for any major Elgar setting. He was Laurence Binyon, and his *The Spirit of England* became the basis of Elgar's 'For the Fallen' (1915–17), one of his greatest and simplest works. Binyon was one of a number of Colvin's colleagues at the British Museum, all of whom became warm friends of the Elgars. To 'Colvin and Colvina', as he affectionately dubbed them, Elgar dedicated his last great work, the Cello Concerto of 1919.

Another husband and wife who stood high in the Elgars' affections were Antonio de Navarro and his wife, the American actress Mary Anderson. De Navarro wanted only to be an English gentleman, and retired early to the Cotswold village of Broadway. His wife, who disliked the life of the stage despite her great talent, was only too happy to turn herself to encouraging and entertaining their friends, who included John Singer Sargent, Henry James, J. M. Barrie, and the Elgars. The de Navarros were Catholic, and during Alice's lifetime especially that was an added bond. The relationship is caught in one of many anecdotes related by Mme. de Navarro in a chapter of her *Memories* devoted to Elgar:

His wit was quick. One evening at Gloucester, during the Three Choirs Festival, we were dining at an hotel; a rope of pearls I was wearing broke and rolled towards him. He looked at them and then, in a pained way, at me: 'Mamie, I always suspected you thought very little of me, but I did not dream that it would come to this.'

Elgar was not one of those who fights shy of new friendships in later life. His magnetism brought him would-be friends from every direction, and to those he could like or love he opened himself freely. Two remarkable and contrasting friendships of his old age show this quality. One was with a woman forty years his junior and entirely unknown to fame. Vera Hockman was a violinist, a member of Billy Reed's orchestra in Croydon when Elgar came there to conduct in 1931. She idolised from afar, but his eye caught hers and he asked to be introduced. He was, as everyone knew, 'susceptible'; but the friendship with Vera almost instantly took on a different dimension. He gave her the copy of Longfellow's *Hyperion* he had shared with his mother. When she came to his home in Worcester to go through the Violin Sonata, he gave her the manuscript sketches for the work. And she became the last of his *'Enigma' Variations*-like inspirations when he labelled the second subject of his incipient Third Symphony 'V. H.'s own theme – will never be finished?' This Symphony was hardly begun before fatal illness overtook Elgar. Yet his embarking on such a project at the age of 75, after more than a dozen years away from major composition, shows with the greatest clarity the power which friendship wielded right to the end of his life.

Bernard Shaw, Elgar, and Vera Hockman at the Hereford Festival, September 1933.

The other friendship of his old age was his only close relationship with a man whose greatness matched his own – Bernard Shaw (1856–1950). It began with an introduction at luncheon near the end of the First World War. Elgar had rejoiced (as who has not?) in the reading of Shaw's early musical criticism. Earlier in his life Elgar had been suspicious of the anti-religious stance of some of Shaw's plays; but by this time, as he was approaching 60, religion meant less to Elgar. What meant much more was intelligent appreciation, and here Shaw made no mystery of his feelings: 'a greater man than I can hope to be', was his public description of Elgar, in his friend's presence, in 1929. They were as different as chalk and cheese – as different as Stanford and Elgar: yet such was the chemistry of the relationship that they reassured one another and enjoyed each other's company from the moment they met. Shaw used the whole of his power to promote Elgar's music in the 1920s when it was threatened with replacement in the popular affection by younger spirits of the brave new world. In 1932 he was instrumental in persuading the B.B.C. to commission Elgar's Third Symphony. For as Shaw had written early in their friendship:

To the north countryman who, on hearing of Wordsworth's death, said, 'I suppose his son will carry on the business' it would be plain today that Elgar is carrying on Beethoven's business. The names are up on the shop front for everyone to read: ELGAR late BEETHOVEN & CO.

Thus the greatest man among Elgar's friends delicately joined the eminence of his final years with the humble origin of the shopkeeper's son. The journey between had been completed with the help and constant reassuring affection of his friends.

Elgar with Ivor Atkins at the Gloucester Festival, 1922.

3

Heroic Vision

Literary Sources

FROM THE TIME Edward Elgar was a baby on his mother's knee, his eldest sister Lucy recalled their mother gathering the children round her to read to them. The poems and stories, some of her own composition, were all carefully chosen to show the children her own view of the world. Lucy wrote of their mother:

Her own young life had been peopled from noble books, and it was in their pages she had met her friends and companions – men romantically honorable and loyal, women faithful in love even unto death; both alike doing nobly with this life because they held it as a gauge of life eternal. And in her simple way of thinking she verily believed these shadowy forms to be portraits of the people whom she would one day meet with in the world . . .

But she had a far greater ability to conceal her disappointments than her famous son would ever discover within himself.

Yet the mother's philosophy contained several notions which were to be fundamental in the life and music of her son. One was the value of the countryside, its cycles of hours and seasons a model for the immortality God intended all His children to look forward to. (The implications for the composer and his music will be explored in Chapter 5.) The way to that immortality – even among the survivors on earth – lay in immersing oneself in the countryside and its lessons. Allied to the countryside was the basic rightness of its social institutions: those who had the land, especially by inheritance, were the people who deserved to have it. (The implications will be discussed in Chapter 8.) For all these things the mother's chosen literature gave both example and dream to her children.

Edward's relationship with his mother was characterised by Hubert Leicester thus:

It was she who peopled the world with heroes and poets for E. and led his mind, which needed only the merest hint of things of beauty . . .

Edward ultimately was inspired and haunted by his mother's vision. This was seriously but not fatally undermined by his father's insecurity and indolence. Together they made a formula for an unhappy life.

One of the favourite poems of mother and children was 'The Better Land' by the popular early nineteenth-century poet Mrs. Hemans:

> 'I hear thee speak of a better land,
> Thou call'st its children a happy band;
> Mother! oh, where is that radiant shore?
> Shall we not seek it, and weep no more?
> Is it where the flower of the orange blows,
> And the fire-flies glance through the myrtle boughs?'
> – 'Not there, not there, my child!'

And so this conversation between son and mother proceeds through several stanzas until the goal is identified beyond the grave. Its lesson was grimly underlined by the deaths of two family sons. Yet it was often the brightness of this world's sights and sounds and scents that drew Edward. Years later he would recall the pungent smell of the fir trees dark in the sunshine surrounding the cottage at Broadheath.

Mother and son were constantly in and out of the bookshops of Worcester. The family rooms above the shop were full of books, and Edward could see his mother at any available moment lay aside her daily cares in favour of reading and even writing – of which she did more as the children grew older. When he was about fifteen, a neighbourhood bookseller rented a loft over one of the Elgar sheds and there stored his overstock. Edward fell upon them, getting up at first light morning after morning to read:

I finished by reading every one of those books – including the theology. The result of that reading has been that people tell me I know more of life up to the eighteenth century than I do of my own time, and it is probably true.

There speaks the son of Ann Elgar, fully aware of the escape from daily care that reading and fantasy hold for their devotees, and more ready to take advantage of that escape than his mother was.

One of his first encounters with a girl was recalled in connection with those books. Practising his violin in the front room above the shop one day, he admired a girl on the pavement below. He invited her up – only to read to her from Voltaire's *Candide*. He was promptly laughed at, and abandoned. But then the favourite book he shared with his mother was Longfellow's prose romance *Hyperion*. It is a romantic traveller's picture of distant lands, where the romance is in the imagination: the one chance for physical bliss is lost when the hero meets a real woman.

Repeatedly he had tried his boyish hand at writing: a childhood play filled with portentous imagery of youth and age; a poem about 'The

Language of Flowers' to present to Lucy on her twentieth birthday; a ghost story (a genre of which he was always fond); reminiscences of various kinds. He was an instinctual writer, to whom spontaneity was everything. Organisation was never his strong point, as his awful struggles to make himself clear in the Birmingham University lectures of later years were to prove.

He was drawn to the pun – the slippery use of one set of words or sounds in multiple meanings. An example of his wit in this genre has already been quoted (p. 26). Another came when his friend W. H. Reed produced a piece called *The Lincoln Imp*, which it was hoped would be popular. 'Well, Billy,' said Elgar, 'I hope it won't make your income limp.' Wit by means of subtle variations in sound is an ability precious to the extemporiser in music. On one occasion the actual crossover was observed by his daughter Carice. When they were staying in Italy for the first time, they came across a village called 'Moglio': Elgar was so amused that he kept rolling this ridiculous word around his tongue until at last it spawned a musical phrase to be used prominently in the Overture *In the South*.

Religious Sources

Ann Elgar brought up her children as Roman Catholics, and she was the centre of their young lives. Lucy recalled:

. . .We felt that if Mother was taken from us, or had a serious illness, or was parted from us for any length of time, the world would be just four bare walls to us – and nothing else! She always held the absolute belief that all which happens to a good person happens for the best . . . and if we put our small helpless hands into the Hands of Compassion, the guiding guarding Hands, we shall be lifted up and strengthened for all we have to do.

That counsel stood them in good stead when Harry died in 1864:

My remembrance of that dread time is like a confused dream. But I seemed to realise even then that when our joys die, they find no grave for us. *We* must live on, just as the rose-tree lives though all its flowers be broken off; and the Spring brings roses again.

And thus Lucy saw her parents 'recompensed' for the loss of their first son by the promise of the second son, 7-year-old Edward.

Perhaps it was after the death of little Jo two years later that Edward's memory was impressed with the ghastly image on an eighteenth-century monument in the northwest corner of Worcester Cathedral. He was to remember it all his life; in old age he took some friends round the Cathedral, and one of them noted:

Pausing before a skull, underneath which are two fearsome wings, he told us how as a little boy the gruesome sight fascinated him, and he still remembered the thrill of fear with which he regarded it.

'The Death of St. Joseph', engraving given by Fr. Waterworth
in September 1868 to the 11-year-old Elgar (*enlarged*).

The Cathedral was the province of his father; W. H. Elgar supplied music to the Cathedral Choir, counted several lay clerks among his close friends, was also friendly with the Cathedral organist, and tuned pianos for many of the Cathedral clergy.

Yet the church of mother and children, and of W. H. Elgar's organistship, was half a mile distant in St. George's Catholic Church. Catholicism was very much a minority faith in an English cathedral city less than half a century after Catholic Emancipation. But the children's education was entirely Catholic – first at a Dame's School in Britannia Square, later for Edward at the Catholic school started by the Berkeley family at Spetchley Park, finally at a well-known Catholic academy at Littleton House run by Francis Reeve (who had himself wanted to be a priest). When Edward began at this last school, the superior priest at St. George's Church gave him a little picture of the sort common among Catholic children then and later. It showed the Death of St. Joseph: was the Jesuit priest thinking of the death of the Elgars' own Jo two years earlier? The legend was in French, easy to translate:

> You Shall Live Again From Out Of The Tomb
> *He Who Believes In Me Shall Never Die*
> and this passing death is nothing but a sleep
> *to make entry into Eternal Life.*

Elgar was to keep this memento carefully all his life, and it is present today at the Cottage in Broadheath.

On the one hand, Edward's attention was brought early to the subject of death and resurrection – through the deaths of his brothers, and through his mother's view of the renewing nature of this world and her Roman Catholic view of the afterlife. Yet on the other hand, his mother wanted her children to achieve things in this world as well. Lucy recalled: 'She wished us to be of the *crew* of this great ship we call the world, and not of its useless passengers.' So while the achievements of this life would certainly be judged, they might not be of any final efficacy. And even this complexity was contradicted by their father's oft-expressed disbelief in what he once called 'the absurd superstition and playhouse mummery of the Papist'. Edward, as the surviving musician among the Elgar sons, would have been especially vulnerable to his father's doubts. These were to emerge in the younger Elgar's life in various ways.

Substituting for his father as organist during Sunday Mass, he whiled away the long sermons with cartoons and doodles of every description in the choir and organ part-books. A little later he spent the sermon time in sketching and writing out pieces for the Wind Quintet to play at their Sunday afternoon meetings. When he himself became organist of the Catholic Church in 1886, he wrote to a friend: 'I am a full fledged organist & – *hate* it.' These were portents for the course of his later life.

At the time of his marriage, his bride was an Anglican. But she supported her husband's Catholic faith and his attendance at Mass, and in a few years became a Catholic herself. She remained faithful lifelong, and there is no doubt that her example and persuasion and support preserved her husband's faith far longer than it might otherwise have lasted. During the 1890s he attended church less frequently – often absent because of compositional pressures which know no Sabbath. From that point onward the fortunes of Elgar's faith can be traced in the subjects he chose for his major religious choral works, his treatment of those subjects, and how they intertwined with the more purely literary heroes for compositions, also of his own choosing.

Knightly Heroes

This was the equipment which Elgar brought to his search through music for an ideal hero, a figure to guide the dreams of his creative life. First among his notable works came the Overture *Froissart* (1890). His inspiration was a generalised world of chivalry long ago and far away. A passage in Sir Walter Scott's *Old Mortality* gave more specific suggestion. The speaker is a Royalist commander addressing a young man puzzled by the conflicting claims of tradition and revolution.

'Did you ever read Froissart? . . . His chapters inspire me with more enthusiasm than even poetry itself. And the noble canon, with what true chivalrous feeling he confines his beautiful expressions of sorrow to the death of the gallant and high-bred knight, of whom it was a pity to see the fall, such was his loyalty to his king, pure faith to his religion, hardihood towards his enemy, and fidelity to his lady-love! – Ah, benedicite! how he will mourn over the fall of such a pearl of knighthood, be it on the side he happens to favour, or on the other. But, truly, for sweeping from the face of the earth some few hundreds of villain churls, who are born but to plough it, the high-born and inquisitive historian has marvellous little sympathy . . .'

Here were romance, elegance, boldness, and social ambition in a heady mixture. The music it engendered is youthful and vibrant, but with a soft nostalgia altogether his own. It was still a generalised picture.

Even a year before *Froissart*, Elgar had begun a choral work which was to add some definition to his image of heroism. It was *The Black Knight* (1889–92), the setting of a German ballad in Longfellow's translation. Here one of the defining themes of Elgar's music makes its first appearance – the hero as outsider. The ballad shows the ordered chivalry of an old kingdom upset by a mysterious stranger dressed in black, who defeats all champions in the lists and then steals the old king's future itself by poisoning the royal children with a magic drink. No explanation is offered, and at the end the Knight says only, 'Roses in the Spring I gather!' It is the outsider who upsets the settled tradition to establish his own power: a magnetic image for a self-taught young composer seeking to blow his trumpet before the wall of social and academic privilege. What is less clearly defined is the appeal to darkness within the hero himself – an element which was to grow constantly through Elgar's major vocal works of the following decade.

Two heroes appeared side by side in works both dating from 1896. One was King Olaf, the only Christian among the Norse saga heroes. Olaf is an outcast seeking to gain his usurped kingdom. The Longfellow poem (from *Tales of a Wayside Inn*) shows a rough old pirate. But Elgar asked his literary neighbour and friend in Malvern, Harry Acworth, to help him mitigate the violent features. The libretto that resulted shows a dreamer whose successes in the political world are only temporary, and who never succeeds with women. At the end only his mother is left to pray for his vision. The subject, in many of its 'Scenes', drew from Elgar music of the most sensitive imagination.

The other hero of 1896 was more specifically Christian. The work was *The Light of Life*, a short oratorio written for the Worcester Festival to a libretto by his Anglican colleague of chamber music in the old days, Edward Capel-Cure. The hero is the blind man healed by Christ. But the healing is only half the story. The second half of the work deals with the rejection of the now sighted – and by implication insighted – man by the mob. So it becomes a parable of the loneliness conferred by vision, especially when the vision is of a minority religion. No wife is in evidence, but once again the hero's mother plays a large role. In terms of real action, she is larger than the hero himself. In the first half the mother boldly argues with Christ for her son's healing and succeeds. In the second half she berates the nay-sayers, showing herself a woman very much in the mould of Ann Elgar. The end is deeply ambiguous, just as in *King Olaf*. In both, the hero has gained his sight and insight at the cost of a place among his fellow men. It is easy enough to apply the moral to Elgar himself, either in his creative life or in his faith. So far the two had not come into clear conflict.

It would be interesting to know whether Elgar was drawn to the subject of his next cantata, *Caractacus* (1898), entirely because of that hero's supposed identification with the Malvern Hills that were also his own home. Or was there also some dark attraction in the surviving scrap of history which showed this hero's utter defeat?

The fragment was in fact so slight that Elgar had to have a story largely manufactured to provide a libretto. He turned again to Harry Acworth to make the verses, but it is clear that the composer himself pulled the strings. Caractacus, an older hero, leads dwindling and beleaguered British forces in the face of the Roman advance. Both his daughter and her Druid lover read disaster in the omens. But the hero is misled by the Arch-Druid, acting from motives never made clear. There are no battles in the foreground of the action, which is entirely taken up throughout the latter half of the work with defeat and captivity. The work shows Elgar himself in some sort of dark crisis (it was the year of the *'Enigma' Variations*). The scenes are larger and more imposing than the *Scenes from the Saga of King Olaf*, but the level of invention is lower.

Private Explorations

The work which followed the *Variations* in 1899 was *Sea Pictures*. This cycle of solo songs with orchestra traces a voyage into the depths of the self. Opening images of night and sleep recall the opening of *Caractacus*. But in *Sea Pictures* there is an unmistakable final triumph in Elgar's music as the lonely spirit of 'The Swimmer' leaps into a seascape of overwhelming challenge, even desolation. That is precisely the heroism required of Elgar's next and greatest hero, Gerontius. And the author of the words of 'The Swimmer' had a double significance for Elgar and his next work: he was a suicide, and his surname was Gordon.

The early history of Elgar's involvement with 'The Dream of Gerontius' was his involvement with the story of General Gordon of Khartoum. It began with the wave of grief and outrage which swept the country after Gordon's strange death in 1885. If the Gladstone government had done nothing to save the beleaguered General, the General himself had seemed to do nothing but court death right up to the moment when he received the native spear front and centre as if he had gone out deliberately to meet it. This was a new conception of heroism – one of those ideas that at first seems so unaccountable, until the persistent fascination of it begins to whisper a suggestion that some new dark place in human nature is in process of being revealed.

Gordon himself had certainly had the personal qualities to plant such an idea. He was a natural brinksman, relying on quick responses and legerdemain to snatch his victories one after another from the jaws of almost certain defeat. That was his trademark, and he became famous for it. But what set the seal on his supreme acceptability to the Victorian conscience was his high Anglicanism: everything he did, he insisted, was the result of inspiration from God precisely as understood by high Anglican orthodoxy. So his every success seemed to validate still further the ideals of England – Church, State, and Empire. Gordon's brand of Anglicanism was next door to Roman Catholicism itself, and the rest of his attributes could offer the young Elgar a powerful model for his own life – hope, insecurity, and the wish to follow his mother's dream and his own.

When Gordon had been about to leave England for what proved the last time, an admiring young man put into his hands a copy of Cardinal Newman's poem 'The Dream of Gerontius'. This little book was with Gordon during his last weeks – right up to the moment he sent the *Times* correspondent back to safety just before the débâcle. The correspondent took with him the little book, and brought it back to England. It found its way to the Birmingham Oratory, where the old Cardinal himself was still alive. It was discovered that the martyred hero of Khartoum had marked many passages of special appeal. At the beginning he had marked the poem's dedication to another Gordon,

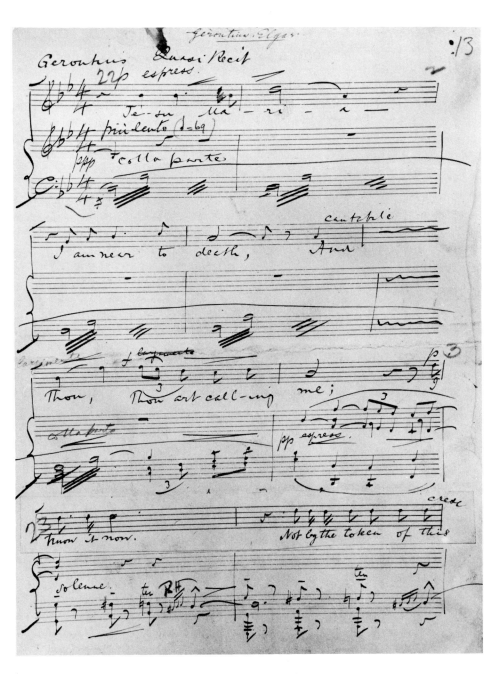

The entry of Gerontius in Part I, *The Dream of Gerontius*
(Elgar's manuscript vocal score).

John Joseph Gordon, a young friend of the Cardinal's who had died high in his affection. The dedication 'Fratri desideratissimo' the later Gordon had underlined as a sign that he had taken it to himself.

The Gordon markings in 'The Dream of Gerontius' made such a sensation at Birmingham that they were circulated from hand to hand throughout the Midlands. Elgar remembered being given a copy of the poem with the Gordon markings added by a priest at St. George's Church in Worcester at the time of his marriage in 1889. But he already knew the Gordon markings, for at the time Alice's mother died in the spring of 1887, Elgar had lent Alice his copy of the poem with the Gordon markings, which she copied into her own book. This was several years before she herself became a Catholic, and it is further evidence of the poem's magnetic effect upon believers and would-be believers there and then.

What fired Elgar's imagination in the Gordon story and the little book associated with it was the special brand of heroism and that heroism's defeat. It was as though he sensed, along with the most prescient of his countrymen, that the day of such self-sacrifice for old ideals was darkening – that the extravagant, lonely heroism of the sort which had touched the Victorian imagination could now hardly be distinguished from suicide. In this, as in much else through the middle decades of his life, Elgar was in the vanguard of reflective thought. It was to account for the rise in the popularity of his most serious works to unprecedented heights during the first decade of the new century, for the continued prescience of his music to the national fortunes and the fortunes of western Europe through the remainder of his career. When his music's popularity declined after 1910, it was not because the music was less prescient, but because the message it was now delivering was unwelcome to its audience.

In the 1890s it was not so. The strange significance of Gordon's death was felt but not understood. It needed interpretation, most of all in a contemplative, evocative art such as music. Elgar's response to the challenge set him on the way toward a great work – a work that would far transcend, as all great works of art do, the circumstances of its conception.

The heroism of Gerontius is divided, like that of the blind man in *The Light of Life*, into two phases. The earlier, earthly phase shows Gerontius (literally 'Old Man') dying – beset by appalling fears, comforted by Catholic 'Assistants' who pray for his soul and a Priest who completes the noble farewell. The longer second part deals with the Soul's progress through the region of 'Demons', and the region of 'Angelicals', to a supreme, instantaneous vision of the Almighty, and relegation to Purgatory. Almost every aspect of this scenario called forth from Elgar great and deeply felt music: the subject is mighty indeed, and no one has ever suggested that Elgar's music is not fully equal to it.

The orchestral Prelude traces a long-drawn pattern of *crescendo-diminuendo* to reveal the leading emotions and many themes to come. The evocation of the terrified, dying hero surrounded by soft prayers of the Assistants, culminating in the peace of farewell and fine dismissal by the awesome Priest, sustains a level of inspiration rarely achieved by any human endeavour but the very greatest. Even Stanford confessed he would have given his head to have written Part I of *Gerontius*.

Part II pursues the Soul's journey with an Angel companion. The solo writing, as in much of Part I, is in long-lined recitative built largely on recurring musical motives. The journey is punctuated by three big choral set-pieces. The first is a furious fantasy and fugue for the Demons, exulting in their ability to mock the Soul's beliefs. This is the only less than compelling section of the score: it has been claimed that Elgar, like César Franck, was unable to evoke real evil in his music. Yet the Demons in *Gerontius* are as they are because they are seen as basically vulgar, incapable of commanding form. Their musical architecture is showy but untoward, like the architecture of Pandemonium in Milton's *Paradise Lost*. Thus the Demons exert no magnetism for the Soul – or for the audience who share his experience. The contrast comes with the extended chorus of Angelicals, 'Praise to the Holiest', where a series of graduated climaxes reveals Elgar's greatness as a creator of big structures. Before the approach to God an awesome heavenly priest, the Angel of the Agony, pleads for the Soul. Judgment comes through a mounting orchestral climax aimed toward a single shattering chord: this was the passage that Jaeger pleaded for, to make a climax even after 'Praise to the Holiest'. The work ends with the companion Angel's farewell turning to soft choral majesty as the Soul sinks slowly beneath the waters of Purgatory. The subject focussed in a single action all of Elgar's hopes and fears for himself and his world. He was never to match this evocation of ideal heroism in any later work of choral or programme music.

Gerontius was said to be a failure at its premiere in the Birmingham Festival of 1900. The bad performance, under Hans Richter, was due partly to the music's advanced idiom, partly to an inadequate rehearsal system backed up by several mischances including the death of the regular chorus-master just before rehearsals commenced, partly to delay in receiving the score through last-minute revisions. Elgar was so distraught that he revealed his own secret doubts in a private letter to Jaeger:

I have worked hard for forty years & at the last, Providence denies me a decent hearing of my work: so I submit – I always said God was against art & I still believe it. Anything obscene or trivial is blessed in this world & has a reward . . .

I am very well & what is called 'fit' & had my golf in good style yesterday & am not ill or pessimistic – don't think it: but I have allowed my heart to open once – it is now shut against every religious feeling & every soft, gentle impulse *for ever*.

**The Dream of Gerontius conducted by
Hans Richter at the Birmingham Festival.**

Those are not, as Ernest Newman once noted, the accents of a man whose faith is firm. Such words raise the speculation that Elgar had poured his best into *Gerontius* in the hope that God would reward him with serene faith for himself – a sort of spiritual wager with the Almighty. When the looked-for triumph did not turn up, the composer's private faith was left on a lower plane than before the work was written.

**Elgar finishing the orchestral score of *Gerontius*
at Birchwood, 3 August 1900: a snapshot
taken by a friend who happened
to arrive at that moment.**

Yet everyone recognised the inherent quality of *Gerontius* – even hard-bitten critics who attended the first performance. The Germans took it up, and after a performance at the Lower Rhine Festival in May 1902 Richard Strauss raised his glass to 'the first English progressivist, Meister Edward Elgar'. Some people have made the ill-natured suggestion that it was not until Germany approved that England acknowledged. That is nonsense: one has only to read the first performance reviews to see how wrong it is. And quite soon, without the experience of the German performances, Birmingham asked Elgar to write a major work for their next Festival in 1903. Elgar accepted.

The 'Apostles' Project

For the new work Elgar turned to an idea he had tried earlier, and then abandoned for lack of time to work it out properly. This was something about the Apostles of Christ, for which he would be ultimately his own librettist and select his own passages and stories from the Bible. So the entire action as well as the music would be of his own making, and reflect its creator. Here he looked for something like final fulfilment.

The origin of the *Apostles* idea had been the old schoolmaster's remark to his pupils at Littleton House: 'The Apostles were poor men, young men at the time of their calling; perhaps before the descent of the Holy Ghost not cleverer than some of you here.' So each of the Apostles, like Gerontius and his predecessors, was an outsider – an outsider whose inspiration might win him an honoured place in the eternal scheme. Yet it was just here that the dark side of Elgar's impulse showed itself paradoxically strongest: his point of entry into the whole subject was the betrayer Judas.

Elgar mitigated the evil of his own doubt as best he could. Searching widely through the commentaries, he found the point of view (well known to theologians) that Judas was not black-hearted but really a misguided enthusiast eager to force Christ to show divine power and thus instantly convert all unbelievers. It had its attractions for the man whose faith was less than perfect: The figure of Judas was to provide Elgar with his strongest point of personal sympathy with the Apostles.

He thought of several possible plans. A visit to Bayreuth in 1902 to see the *Ring* operas of Wagner persuaded him to plan a trilogy of oratorios. As he got down to it this seemed too much, especially with the Birmingham Festival of 1903 now only a year away. So he reduced the plan to a large single work. For help with the libretto he turned again to Capel-Cure, the Anglican clergyman who had done the libretto for *The Light of Life*. Capel-Cure provided valuable suggestions and sketches to meet Elgar's ideas with compilations from diverse passages in Scripture. But he jibbed at Elgar's idea of Judas, and Elgar looked elsewhere for help. He found a sympathetic spirit in another Anglican, Canon C. V. Gorton of Morecambe (whom he knew through the Canon's musical competition festival).

Anglicans were more useful than Catholics, Elgar reasoned, if he wanted to avoid the doctrinal trouble which beset *Gerontius* in several English cathedrals, and appeal to the widest audience. In abandoning the Catholic viewpoint, however, Elgar abandoned one of his strongest points of identification with religion. In any case, Gorton proved a more pacific counsellor, and later wrote pamphlets endorsing the theology of Elgar's libretto.

Elgar also looked for help to literature – specifically to his mother's favourite poet Longfellow (whose works had provided the libretto for *The Black Knight* and most of *King Olaf*). In Longfellow's works he found 'The Divine Tragedy', a long versification of many phases in Christ's life on earth. Here was a single story of actual conversion: Longfellow's example was not one of the twelve Apostles but Mary Magdalene, identified with the woman who had washed Christ's feet with her tears. Conversion must clearly be a central matter in any work about the Apostles. Yet Elgar was so uncertain of himself in this matter that he accepted the suggestion of a figure from outside the twelve Apostles for his conversion-story. A third figure, to lead the Apostles after the Crucifixion, would be Peter. So the plan evolved for an oratorio in three parts.

Elgar began his music with a brief and deeply felt choral Prologue; a long scene of Christ's meditation in the garden at night; a spectacular orchestral sunrise; and the calling of the Apostles. A pastoral second scene showed Christ instructing the Apostles in the Beatitudes, with characteristic individual reactions from the leading figures. All of this provided more than half an hour of finely inspired music, full of master-strokes but as yet unclear in direction. It was a lack of clarity which was to pursue the entire work to its ambiguous end.

For instead of planning his action and libretto thoroughly before beginning the music, as Wagner had done, Elgar's method was to develop the libretto and music side by side, often allowing the music to lead his mind before any words were fixed upon. Elgar's beginning for Judas, for instance, had been a fragment of instrumental music – for all the world as if Judas were another 'Enigma' Variation. (That figure, written down in 1899, was ultimately used for the Angel of the Agony in *Gerontius* – a telling equation.) The result of this method of simultaneous construction of music and libretto was an extraordinary dependence on the fits and starts of inspiration. It was late February 1903 before he was ready to begin on the first major portrait among his three *Apostles* characters, Mary Magdalene. The premiere of the whole work was scheduled at Birmingham for October. It left less than eight months to complete the entire score from sketches, orchestrate it, supervise the printing, choose soloists, and rehearse.

The character of Mary Magdalene was complex in Longfellow's poem. She had to wait for conversion upon events outside herself. During what was to be Mary Magdalene's process of thought toward conversion, Longfellow made her observe Peter's efforts to walk over the water to Christ. Elgar seized on this for his libretto: by masking the thought process of his central character at the crucial moment, he could mask his own lack of certain understanding. Later, during the time of her symbolic long journey in search of Christ, Elgar himself introduced an entirely unrelated incident – Peter's recognition of Christ. No doubt it was good preparation for the Peter section to come. But again it obscured direct understanding of the central matter – just as Elgar, if left to his own devices three years earlier, would not have taken the listener anywhere near the presence of the Almighty in *Gerontius*. The

Mary Magdalene scene in *The Apostles* is long and heavy with expectation of an inspiration that never really arrives. We are told that Mary Magdalene believes, and we are shown the spectacle of washing Christ's feet. But like the composer, we wait in vain for conviction. It is the only fundamentally unsuccessful part of *The Apostles*. Unfortunately it is central.

Elgar's realisation of the misguided betrayer Judas, by contrast, is a complete success. Here is yet another case of heroism in two parts. First comes the man of action, to make his bargain and do the job. Then, against the Temple singers' rendition of the bloodthirsty 94th Psalm, Judas hovers outside and applies the cruel words of the Psalm to himself, realises the enormity of what he has done, and resolves suicide. Judas is the most compelling character-study in the whole range of Elgar's music – the ultimate outsider.

The Betrayal brings on the Crucifixion (hardly noticed in Elgar's music) and then a vast ensemble of increasing choral climaxes to depict the Ascension. The accomplishment here outdoes even 'Praise to the Holiest' in *Gerontius*, and it is as fine as anything Elgar ever wrote.

Longdon Marsh, near Birtsmorton, where Elgar went many times as he worked out 'The Ascension' music in *The Apostles*: a photograph by Elgar himself, 1903.

But again he was behind schedule. At the end of June 1903 he confessed to the publishers and the Festival authorities that he could not complete the Peter music in time. Everyone was very nice about it, as there was already more than two hours of music. The performance at Birmingham in October 1903 was a complete success. So Elgar reverted to his trilogy plan: only now, the Peter sketches would make a basis for beginning the Apostles' work on earth. This next instalment, ultimately called *The Kingdom*, was planned for the next Birmingham Festival in October 1906.

The major works of the intervening years, *In the South* (1904) and the *Introduction and Allegro* (1905), showed contrasting landscapes abroad and nearer home. Both perhaps hinted at Elgar's wish to escape from the toils of the half-formed *Apostles* plan to which he had committed himself. Another sign of the wish to escape was his acceptance of the Professorship of Music at the new University of Birmingham late in 1904. It was not a post for which he was fitted by background or temperament. When his University appointment extended into the beginning work on his new oratorio, *The Kingdom*, for the next Birmingham Festival, he announced in a lecture:

I still look upon music which exists without any poetic or literary basis as the true foundation of our art . . . No arguments I have yet read have altered this view.

What then of *The Kingdom*? The end of 1905 found Elgar, worried and unhappy, working up his sketches for the Peter section originally planned for the first *Apostles*. These Peter sketches went back to 1902, and they contained inspired ideas. They were to make an early focus for the new work, centred on the Pentecostal descent of holy fire, the speaking in tongues. Later he had the notion of a big solo for the grieving, exulting Mary – the most eloquent of all the mothers in his music – set against an orchestral sunset of brilliant colours fading to dusk. This was sketched amid great inner turmoil, for the basic impulse had been lost. When he tried to push the music farther into real action – that is, significantly beyond what he had planned in 1902–3 – the effort brought him to the verge of nervous collapse. *The Kingdom*, as realised for the Birmingham Festival of 1906, was a half hour shorter than *The Apostles* of 1903 and contained little more than the Peter music originally planned for Part III of the earlier work.

When the hero was faced with the necessity for real action, he and his composer failed. It was an indication of why, though Elgar widely advertised his interest in writing an opera and was offered tempting propositions by distinguished writers from Thomas Hardy downward, all the opera ideas came to nothing. Of all the heroes and heroines in *The Apostles* and *The Kingdom*, only Christ instructing the Apostles and Judas reflecting on the smash of his schemes are real individuals. The survivors in *The Kingdom* are unable to look forward to any positive action: they use up their fragile energies merely contemplating the past. A year after *The Kingdom* premiere, Elgar realised he would never complete the trilogy.

Elgar with sketches of *The Kingdom*, Plas Gwyn, winter 1905–06.

Ironies

The doom of the *Apostles* project was the making of the Symphonies and Violin Concerto (1908–11). In these works Elgar could look forward and backward at will through his music, unhampered by any 'poetic or literary basis'. But during those years when his greatest talents came into full focus, his own literary abilities created minor counterpoint in several sets of verses for his own music.

First came a poem for the last in a set of four part songs composed at the end of 1907. The cycle had begun in the warmth of Tennyson's 'Lotos-Eaters', dimmed to the sepulchral lamp of Byron's 'Deep in my Soul', cooled in Shelley's 'Ode to the West Wind'. For a finale, Elgar made verses of deathly chill entitled 'Owls':

What is that? Nothing.
The leaves must fall, and falling, rustle;
That is all:
They are dead
As they fall, –
Dead at the foot of the tree;
All that can be is said.
What is it? Nothing.

The recurring 'Nothing', he wrote to Jaeger, is only 'an *owlish* sound'.
The poem is subtitled 'An Epitaph'. It was a forecast of the nullity that
would overtake his own creative life when age and war and loss had
marked him too deeply.

Yet this poem preceded the great symphonic works of 1908–11. Their
achievement signalled a flaming up of desire in a landscape however
barren. Between the composition of the First Symphony and the Violin
Concerto, in the winter of 1909–10, Elgar wrote two solo songs to his
own words: 'Paraphrases of Eastern Folk Songs' he called them, to
detach the towering passion of their words from autobiography. (The
'adaptations', he said, were by 'Pietro d'Alba' – alias his daughter
Carice's pet Peter Rabbit.) But the autobiography is there. 'Dark is the
wood, The track's ever lonely and grey,' sings the lover in *The Torch* in
an echo of *Owls*. In the other song-words of his own composition, *The
River* is seen first as a life-giving mother, then as a traitorous mistress:
'Wounded and alone I stand, Tricked, derided, impotent!'

After the Second Symphony in 1911, Elgar attempted to focus all the
conflicting elements of his heroic vision in a choral ode on Arthur
O'Shaughnessy's *The Music Makers*. This work has always been a
subject of special pleading amongst devotees of Elgar's music. The verse
is largely undistinguished, descending sometimes to bathos. But its
sentiments fitted Elgar's view of the world so exactly that it was
inevitable he should set them. He wrote:

In interpreting O'Shaughnessy's Ode, I have felt that his 'music makers' must
include not only poets and singers but all artists who feel the tremendous
responsibility of their mission to 'renew the world as of yore'.

As I have felt, so I have insisted on this responsibility, therefore the
atmosphere of the music is mainly sad; but there are moments of enthusiasm,
and bursts of joy occasionally approaching frenzy; moods which the creative
artist suffers in creating or in contemplation of the unending influence of his
creation.

Yes, suffers: – this is the only word I dare to use; for even the highest ecstasy of
'making' is mixed with the consciousness of the sombre dignity of the eternity of
the artist's responsibility.

Here was the contradiction exposed for all to see and feel – the sadness of
nostalgia, the hope for art to turn the sadness and disinheritance to
supreme power. Through a warm glow of Edwardian afternoon, when
artists like Elgar were welcomed by Kings and Prime Ministers, that

Carice with Peter Rabbit ('Pietro d'Alba'), Plas Gwyn, *c.* 1907.

hope seemed just tenable. In the second year of a new reign, two years away from the war that would destroy the civilisation of the old world, Elgar knew in his heart it was no good. The new themes inspired by O'Shaughnessy's verses were so far behind the themes Elgar was quoting from his own past works as illustrations in the score that the result was like a row of gorgeous beads strung too loosely on a fragile thread. In the end *The Music Makers* has no heroic message to deliver beyond the vanity of dreams.

Elgar's next major work was the 'symphonic study' *Falstaff* (1913), and here was a message with a vengeance. Heroism was grown old and fat and corrupt. The composer wrote an accompanying essay, revealing how closely the music follows the Falstaff scenes in Shakespeare's *Henry IV* plays, and insisting on Falstaff's nobility still. It was like his laundering of Judas. But in the attempt to twist Falstaff to this purpose, Elgar upset for once the diatonic basis of his own musical style. Falstaff as man and actor is shown in predominantly chromatic terms, leaving the old diatonic heroism for his young friend Prince Hal – King Henry V to be. In this 'study' Falstaff wheedles the young man's affection, covers himself with disgrace at Gad's Hill, chases sluts at the Boar's Head Tavern, and raises a rat-bitten army of mercenaries and wastrels for battle. Only during the two pastoral interludes which Elgar inserted into the action does this anti-hero recall for fleeting moments the dignity and dream of *Froissart* (1890). In less than a quarter century Elgar had travelled the entire gamut of experience from his dearest hopes to despair and the old hero's utter rejection by the future.

Ghosts

The rest of the tale is soon told. In the war years his vision of heroism divided itself between the elegy of Laurence Binyon's *Spirit of England* poems and the childhood escapism of Algernon Blackwood's *The Starlight Express* (a stage realisation, albeit imperfect, of something astonishingly close to the play with music planned in his own childhood with his family). Blackwood was a master of the ghost story, a genre which appealed to Elgar more and more strongly as he aged. After the valedictory chamber music and Cello Concerto of 1918–19, and the death of his wife in 1920, he wrote little more. In 1923 he was persuaded to write incidental music for Binyon's drama *Arthur*, a work hollow and haunting by turns.

Two poems for music show Elgar's world in ruins. One is called *The Wanderer* – adapted, so he claimed, from Restoration verse:

> With a knight of ghosts and shadows
> I summoned am to tourney:
> Ten leagues beyond
> The wide world's end
> Methinks it is no journey.

The other poem is a wraith of marching-song written under the pseudonym 'Richard Mardon'. It is based on the repeating rhythm of the single syllable 'Zut':

> Come! shall we forget our old-time march song?
> The lads sang it so, long long ago . . .

So the vision of a heroism which could be achieved through music serving specific causes died as it faced the modern world. There remained the ideal of absolute music, which Elgar realised through his ultimate instrument, the orchestra.

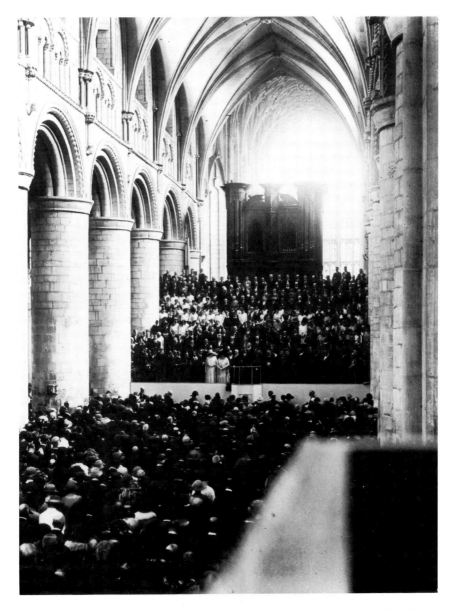

The Kingdom **conducted by Elgar at the Three Choirs Festival,
Gloucester, September 1922.**

Elgar in the midst of a rehearsal at Hastings, *c.* 1922. The photograph is one of very few to catch something of the animation in Elgar's face when the interpretation pleased him – one of his most valuable assets as a conductor of his own music.

4

Orchestra: the ideal medium

ELGAR'S ATTRACTION to ensembles of instruments began almost with the child's interest in music itself. The piano might be more ready to hand. Singers might be easier to find. But almost any ensemble of instruments offered a greater variety of colours and harmonic possibilities. For Elgar, as for all the leading composers of his generation – Richard Strauss, Puccini, Mahler, Sibelius, Debussy, Janáček, Delius – one of the musical horizons was orchestral colour: those who were drawn to it had a natural advantage in developing the music of their day. With Elgar, colour and harmony were almost the same thing. He expressed it thus in a professorial lecture at Birmingham University in 1906:

The modern orchestra is capable of an unending variety of *shades of tone*, not only in succession, but in combination. We see that a whole world of new harmonies is at the disposal of a composer for orchestra: harmonies which may sound execrable and impossible on the piano but which may give the greatest pleasure when scored for instruments. To give a single instance: the dissonant notes of a chord may be merely suggested by the soft-toned instruments, or they may be thundered out by the heavy-toned ones, while the principal notes of the chord – the backbone – is merely suggested. Every shade of every dynamic force is possible for every note of every chord, and this simultaneously. We have only touched on the fringes of the possibilities of modern harmony . . .

Experiments

The notion of using instruments to explore possibilities of harmony went back to the beginning of Elgar's musical life. As a boy he had mastered the piano with brilliant results. But the piano was the symbol of his father's trade – of all the lower middle class limitations he could hope to avoid in his own life. The organ had more sustaining power, but even its range of colour was insufficient for him. It is remarkable indeed that the boy's first sustained attempt at composition, at the age of 12 or

**The only known photograph
of Elgar with his violin,
c. 1885.**

13, was conceived for an ensemble of instruments to be played by his sisters and brother while he himself directed the dramatic action.

One of the instruments, a three-stringed double bass to provide an harmonic foundation for the ensemble, was actually built by Edward himself especially for the purpose. And as this was to be played by his little brother Frank, he devised one of the movements to repeat over and over the notes of the three open strings of the instrument: little Frank had only to saw at each of the strings in order without troubling to finger them, and Edward's music would have its bass foundation. It was a first success in designing a part for a player for whom it was intended. Everything about the endeavour looked forward to the man and artist to come.

The elaborate plan for this play with music was conceived as a vehicle for the purpose of casting the family into an ideal ensemble to function under his own direction – just as he would use the ensemble of the orchestra in maturity. Ultimately the sheer elaboration of the childish plan doomed it, and the play was never produced. But the music stayed with its composer for nearly forty years until, at a crucial moment in his creative life, it made a remarkable reappearance as *The Wand of Youth* – to be described in its place in this chapter.

The matter of elaboration had its own place in Elgar's creative development. It reappeared in his maturity when he was haunted by religious doubts, in the shape of the planned trilogy of oratorios to rival Wagner's *Ring of the Nibelung*. There once again the complication was to prove too great.

The ideal means to elaboration came for Elgar not in shaping his music to plots and stories already existing, but in the purely abstract drama of theme and contrast and form. There again the big orchestra offered his ideal medium. With a single exception, all his greatest works were to be found along that pilgrim path.

At the Worcester Festival rehearsal in September 1869, when he was 12, he heard the orchestra playing the introduction to 'O Thou that tellest' from Handel's *Messiah*. He was so struck by the scoring for all the first and second violins to sound the melody in unison amid the rest of the ensemble that he ran home, borrowed a violin from his father's shop, and began to teach himself to play it. From that moment he never again looked seriously at the piano as more than an aid to composition. The violin would become his means of leading an orchestra – and so, eventually, of conducting it.

More immediately the boy's violin, once he had begun to master it, gave him orchestral experience round the city. His father took him to join in the 'instrumental nights' at the Glee Club, which included movements from Haydn and Beethoven Symphonies. When one of the touring opera companies would put up for a week at the old theatre and recruit its tiny orchestra locally, the boy was sometimes taken into it: they played established favourites like Bellini's *Norma* and Verdi's *Il trovatore*, but Edward's favourite was Mozart's masterpiece *Don Giovanni*. Later, he joined his father in both of the larger orchestras giving concerts in the city, and in the locally recruited orchestra for the Worcester meetings of the Three Choirs Festival once every third year.

Gradually he made acquaintance with the repertoire – or as much of it as the conservative taste of Worcester would programme. The old Cathedral organist, who conducted one of the local orchestras as well as the Worcester Festival, found Mendelssohn acceptable but Schumann incomprehensible. Edward passionately disagreed. Whenever he could gather sufficient money, he began to take himself to the Crystal Palace concerts in London, where August Manns programmed not only Schumann but Berlioz and Wagner. The few violin lessons he took from an eminent teacher, Adolph Pollitzer, only confirmed his interest in the orchestra.

In 1876, when he was 19, he won the post of 'Leader and Instructor' for the new Amateur Instrumental Society being formed in the city. This involved not only some knowledge of repertoire, but enough familiarity with each and every instrument to be able to give at least rudimentary instruction to any player. It was invaluable experience.

Then, with his brother Frank, the Leicesters, and another friend, he formed a woodwind quintet. They had two flutes, oboe, clarinet, and to provide a bass Edward learned the bassoon (another demonstration of his interest in harmonic control). He was also the tireless arranger of music for this original combination, and soon he was composing music for them. The wind quintet music was experimental: very little of it sounds like the mature Elgar to come. But in it the young composer addressed two problems. First he sought to achieve the greatest possible variety from limited means: of all the orchestral choirs, the woodwind offers the greatest variety of instrumental colours – clearly a vital concern for a composer aspiring after composition in large forms. Second, young Elgar pursued the matter of larger form in the wind quintets, enlarging and enlarging the scale of the movements until he achieved structures of between three and four hundred bars.

In 1879 he gained his first conducting job – with an orchestra of attendants at the County Lunatic Asylum at Powick. The attendants' orchestra was to provide entertainment and dances for the patients – an early form of music therapy. Part of the conductor's job was to arrange the music – and, often, to write it. But the ensemble of instruments available depended entirely on what the Asylum personnel of the moment happened to play. Thus the constitution of the band could vary from week to week, and was at the best (in Elgar's own word) 'eccentric'. A typical Powick ensemble contained flute, clarinet, two cornets, euphonium and bombardon (members of the tuba family), two violins, and piano. Amongst these he would have to strike some balance and variety, while seeing that each player had something interesting to play commensurate with his abilities.

The woodwind quintet, *c.* 1879: Frank Exton, flute (*front left*); Frank Elgar, oboe; (*rear, left to right:*) William Leicester, clarinet; Edward Elgar, bassoon; Hubert Leicester, flute.

The need to keep the Powick music entertaining afforded little scope for serious exploration of form. The young Elgar tried to remedy this by studying scores and by opening his ears to whatever repertoire was undertaken by the orchestras in which he played. He also attempted to do something more active: in the programme of the Worcester Festival of 1878 was Mozart's G minor Symphony. The experience of participating in the performance gave the 21-year-old Elgar an idea:

I . . . ruled a score for the same instruments and with the same number of bars as Mozart's G minor Symphony, and in that framework I wrote a symphony, following as far as possible the same outline in the themes and the same modulation. I did this on my own initiative, as I was groping in the dark after light, but looking back after thirty years I don't know any discipline from which I learned so much.

Interest in large form and large ensemble went hand in hand for Elgar, as he was to observe in his creative maturity:

Larger works have demanded larger orchestras, or larger orchestras have demanded larger works. I leave it to historians to decide, if it be worth discovering, which force was the moving power.

Yet it was to be another decade and more before his own large works began to emerge. He spent those years teaching (which he hated), playing the violin (which interested him less and less), conducting (which interested him more and more), and writing a succession of short pieces containing often striking ideas, skilful orchestration, and no attempt at big form.

If Elgar had died in his early thirties, as Schubert did, he would have been forgotten today. If he had died at 35, as Mozart did, he would have been recalled in specialist books on English musical history as a minor composer. He was in fact almost the latest to develop of all the great composers. The entire decade of the 1880s, which saw him out of his twenties and into his thirties, was without significant creative issue for him because one vital item in the equation he needed was missing – the constant companionship and moral support of a wife. When that was supplied, his major works began to flow.

Froissart Overture

First of all came an orchestral overture. Elgar had received an invitation to write a short orchestral work for the Worcester Festival to be held in September 1890. Though he had never written an orchestral work of more than five minutes' length, he determined that this was to be an overture of at least twelve minutes. The difference in scope is great, for as length increases, the complexity needed to hold the music together rises geometrically. Through the spring of 1890, a year after his marriage and in the weeks leading up to his thirty-third birthday, Elgar wrestled with his *Froissart* Overture. His wife (pregnant with their only child), gave him every encouragement.

The new Overture brimmed with ideas. Several were interrelated, others quite independent; but most were presented and re-presented without significant change. The sheer melodic, harmonic, and rhythmic quality of the ideas was superb. Their sequence of presentation in exposition and recapitulation was striking and absorbing, romantic and ardent to match the general subject of medieval chivalry. The middle development section was weak, because Elgar still had little notion of using a long form to invest his music with a gradually growing richness of experience.

Froissart Overture: the opening page of Elgar's full score, 1890.

The scoring was resourceful and idiosyncratic. The basic presentation and argument of ideas was confided to the strings. Woodwind were used not so much for contrast as for subtlety: as with all of Elgar's mature work, there was constant doubling of instruments, and constant variety in that doubling. In the provincial orchestras of Elgar's young days and for a long time afterwards, the standards of instrumental playing were such that it was not always safe to entrust a long solo to anybody: there was safety in numbers. Schumann had treated his orchestra in this way for the same reason. But even the Elgar of *Froissart* was a much more resourceful orchestrator than Schumann, and he varied his doublings constantly to provide accents and shifting colours through the woodwind especially. The brass instruments were used at this early stage largely for reinforcement and brilliance.

The premiere of the *Froissart* Overture, a month after the birth of Elgar's daughter, was conducted by the composer. The reception was generally favourable. A few of the younger musicians recognised its mastery more clearly. One was Ivor Atkins, a dozen years younger than Elgar, a few years later to become organist of Worcester Cathedral. He had never seen Elgar or heard a note of his music before the night of the *Froissart* premiere. But he instantly felt the power that would take Elgar's music to a breadth of public response unknown to any British composer for centuries:

I knew that Elgar was the man for me, I knew that I completely understood his music, and that my heart and soul went with it.

As yet Atkins and a few others were isolated voices. The more conservative composers of the English academic establishment and their pupils did not trouble themselves about this self-taught provincial outsider. And the outsider himself had no faith in his own future. He had boldly taken his bride to live in London, in the vaguest hopes of some undefined recognition. But until *Froissart* appeared, he had written nothing to recognise. In the end he found himself so entirely unknown in London that he could not even find any violin pupils. Circumstances thus forced the Elgars to go back to Worcestershire. They established their home in Malvern, where he took up once again the hated burden of teaching.

Developments

For the next ten years and more Elgar's major compositions would be largely choral, because the Midlands were full of choral societies and choral festivals, and it was the way to get on. And there was another reason. For the self-taught composer who wants to project his music on the largest scale, the conquest of big form is very difficult in music without a programme (as *Froissart* had shown, despite its generalised literary allusion). A plot or libretto solves half the problem of structure before any music is begun. Thus it was in the choral works of the 1890s that Elgar really discovered his mastery of large forms. Occasional orchestral works, representing the silver thread of what he really wanted in music, show themselves in the whole chronology as isolated flashes of brilliance. But they are masterpieces every one.

First, in 1892, came a little Serenade for Strings. The three short movements may well have been based on earlier sketches. But the sheer quality of the delicate ideas, the superb understanding of string writing, and the linking of themes in gentle cycles of formal return mark the Serenade as a work of distinction. It soon became a favourite with players and audiences alike, and it has never lost its place in the repertoire.

No major orchestral piece appeared until the end of the 1890s, but one work of 1895 must be mentioned in any consideration of Elgar's orchestral writing. This is the big Organ Sonata written for Worcester Cathedral in that year. Elgar had been asked for a voluntary. He fulfilled the request with his first really large-scaled instrumental piece in four movements. The Organ Sonata is symphonic in everything but orchestration, and it shows clearly where its composer's mind was tending. The score is full of orchestral ideas and dynamics. It is a rare organist even today who can bring to it the necessary combination of virtuosity and the command of large phrasing and shaping usually found only in conductors.

The Organ Sonata shows that by 1895 Elgar had the ability to project himself through an imposing four-movement structure. He already talked of writing a symphony. But symphony-writing was regarded (in the words of Bernard Shaw, one of the most distinguished music critics of the day), as the 'top department of instrumental music'.

Even in 1898, at the age of 41, Elgar lacked the assurance to address the symphony directly, though he had an invitation to write one for the Worcester Festival. What he produced instead was a set of orchestral variations. The advantage over 'symphonic' form was clear: with variations one could divide the making of a big abstract form into two separate stages: first make the individual variations in any order, and then order these completed fragments into a satisfying sequence. In symphonic writing of larger movements, the two things had to be addressed simultaneously.

The *'Enigma' Variations* were at first shaped out of Elgar's private friendships. But he only craved attention finally for the *Variations'* status as pure music – and rightly. The members of any audience today who can claim to have known any of Elgar's 'friends pictured within' these variations written between eighty and ninety years ago must be fewer and fewer declining to none. Yet the *Variations* remains Elgar's most popular work, a firm fixture in the repertoire of most orchestras.

Its form begins to unfold in a theme ('Enigma') of two separate, even opposite, ideas: one in G minor, the other in G major; one of triple rhythmic suggestion, the other of quadruple actuality; one whose figure leaps, while the other steps. Each of the succeeding variations examines both, combining them in different ways. But the real solution – to combine the two in a single extended melody – is reserved for the Finale. It was a portent for the future. In the last notes of the *Variations* Finale coda, Elgar quite unconsciously foreshadowed the notes of the 'great beautiful tune' (as his wife described it) which was to lead him to the achievement of his first Symphony nine years later.

Orchestration took on the character of a natural setting in the cycle of songs for solo contralto and orchestra, *Sea Pictures*, which followed the *Variations* in 1899. The lone voice pitted against the immense resources of the orchestra here becomes a symbol of the single spirit battling against overwhelming odds of nature. And so Elgar's growing skill as an orchestrator was made a metaphor of deepening personal experience, where battles were fought within a world of interior landscape.

Two attempts to write a symphony both resulted in concert overtures of 1901 and 1904. *Cockaigne (In London Town)* used formal proportions similar to those in *Froissart* to far greater effect. In *Cockaigne* the exposition was treated as a series of variations: each had been brought to Elgar's mind by some place or sound of London. But as with the *Variations*, when these associations had served their turn, he wished the music to be heard with only the vaguest specific ties to the real world. The variations continued to unfold through the *Cockaigne* development: one of them, scored with subtle wit, evokes a Salvation Army band, complete with tambourine, beginning its hymn in two different keys. In the recapitulation, Elgar's growing mastery of form led him to some rearrangement and the deft concision which always makes for compelling listening.

The city picture in *Cockaigne* was followed three years later by an altogether bigger structure to evoke in generous, nostalgic proportions the composer's first experience of the Italian countryside, *In the South*. But the evocation was also of dark, windy weather and the remains of Roman militarism. The profuse and heavy character of the orchestration has often been compared to Richard Strauss, and there was more than a little of Strauss in the gigantism of formal proportions. *In the South*, demanding twenty minutes' playing time, was by far Elgar's biggest orchestral movement up to the time of its composition in 1904. It shows clearly his frustrated desire for the Symphony. But one more remarkable piece was to intervene before he achieved his symphonic goal.

Reminiscence

This was the *Introduction and Allegro* of 1905; which brought to the surface of his consciousness a remarkable habit of mind already foreshadowed in *Sea Pictures, Cockaigne,* and *In the South*. In each of these earlier works, the musical idea which is known to have begun the composition is used neither as first nor as second subject. First and second subjects are both evolved from the original idea, which is then presented some distance into the musical argument (in both the later Overtures it comes between the first and second subjects). No programme note made clear which was the original, nuclear idea which generated all the rest. That knowledge has emerged in modern times only through discoveries of manuscript sketches and the collation of hints dropped casually by Elgar in the course of interviews. In the case of the *Introduction and Allegro* of 1905, however, the composer himself wrote a programme note which revealed this very idiosyncratic cast of mind:

Elgar at work in his study, *c.* **1905.**

Some three years ago, in Cardiganshire, I thought of writing a brilliant piece for string orchestra. On the cliff, between blue sea and blue sky, thinking out my theme, there came up to me the sound of singing . . . Fitting the need of the moment I made the tune which appears in the Introduction and in the coda of this work . . .

The sketch was forgotten until a short time ago, when it was brought to my mind by hearing, far down our own Valley of the Wye, a song similar to those so pleasantly heard [in Cardiganshire] . . . This I have now completed . . .

The 'Welsh' figure was used largely in the *Introduction* (though not at the beginning) and in the coda at the end of the *Allegro*. Thus its occurrence in the music could enact the passage of time – and of subconscious thinking – out of which Elgar made his music. Once again in the *Introduction and Allegro*, all the themes are developed from the one origin. The original idea is there, but it is not placed first because it was not the entity which opened the actual form of the music: its variant did that.

There is always a tension between idea and form in Elgar's music – in part, no doubt, the result of self-teaching. But it is this tension which may explain why Elgar's music has survived where that of his more academic English contemporaries has not. He might *adapt* his thematic thinking *toward* a traditional form, but he would never allow his invention to be governed by the thought of the form. That is why the countryside could play such a role in Elgar's art. Opening up an accepted form to place a 'parental' memory between the two 'children' assigned to carry the burden of formal argument, Elgar's music could be made to enact the very idiosyncratic psychological process by which the ruminative thinking over his original idea could be shaped gradually toward the classic forms in which his music sought its fulfilment. It could be seen as the child of Broadheath making his way in the world. The form is there, employed with irreproachable correctness and sophistication; yet at a certain moment that form is made to pause and pay tribute to the natural, almost wild impulse which lies at the very bottom of the music, and which ultimately gives Elgar's music its strength and character.

The *Introduction* opens with a striking figure derived from the original 'Welsh' idea, leading to the 'Welsh' idea itself. The *Allegro* is made largely of other derivatives; only in the coda does the 'Welsh' idea reappear, singing triumphantly of itself and all its rich progeny. Thus the whole work is psychologically related to the *Variations*, where the two fragments at the beginning lead ultimately to the linkage in a great melody, which is the true theme, at the end.

In this cast of mind, it seems to me, we come close to the essence of Elgar as a composer. The outstanding character of his musical individuality might be described as nostalgia – the nostalgia which can recognise some quality after the original experience itself has passed. Only when it can be recalled, and thereby surrounded with the special atmosphere of things once real but now made precious because of imagination and memory, can the final value be recognised, brought up to the level of consciousness, and shared. It was that recognition, I think, which finally released his long-desired Symphony.

Symphony

Elgar's First Symphony came in 1907–8, three years after the *Introduction and Allegro*. It is built around a 'great beautiful tune' which sounds at the beginning and end of the work, and out of which virtually all of the intervening material is varied. In the Symphony the theme comes right at the beginning – signifying perhaps the bringing of the process at last to full consciousness. Yet the evolution of the Symphony's 'motto' theme (as Elgar himself called it) in the month of the composer's fiftieth birthday provides another fable of his nature and his genius.

Many years afterward it was noticed by W. H. Reed that the opening notes of the Symphony's 'motto' theme had been foreshadowed precisely in the closing notes of the *'Enigma' Variations* coda:

[I] called Elgar's attention to this strange fact on one occasion, pointing out that it was not just a similar passage such as one often meets in comparing the works of any composer with one another, but an *exact* repetition of the theme subconsciously written [eight] years previously, the relative note-values, the intervals *and the accompanying harmony* being identical. The whole theme is transposed into A flat major for the Symphony. Elgar confessed that he was at a loss to account for it, being quite unaware that the repetition existed until it was pointed out to him.

The Symphony's motto theme is essentially a two-part counterpoint. And more recently I discovered the *bass* notes of the 'motto' counterpoint in a prominent phrase of the hero's first and most imposing solo in *King Olaf* (1896): again the harmonic progression is identical, this time in the very tonality of Ab major. So the 'invention' of 1907 was in essence the bringing together in polyphony of two ideas which had existed quite separately in Elgar's thinking for more or less a decade.

What brought them together in the month of the composer's fiftieth birthday – the anniversary before all others which may bring a man to begin to evaluate his life's achievement? However it happened, in that month Elgar's mind was certainly running on the past of his own art. He decided to look out the little tunes he had written for the children's family play nearly forty years earlier, to finish and orchestrate them to the standard of his mature, sophisticated music. Now they were given a significant collective title: *The Wand of Youth*.

***overleaf*: The opening 'motto' theme of the First Symphony, manuscript full score, 1908.**

Going back to scrutinise a distant private past is some evidence of a creative crisis. At such a moment, the creative spirit might naturally return to the basis of its own teaching. Elgar had no formal teaching as a composer, so he could only look at these earliest of all his own compositions. If they were still viable as ideas, to be tested and presented in 'modern dress' so to speak, the basis would be sound. And so it was. The first *Wand of Youth* Suite, finished in the summer of 1907 (between the invention of the Symphony's motto theme and the writing of the Symphony itself) met with great success when given its premiere at the end of the year. But by then Elgar himself was in Italy again – seeking the atmosphere which had produced his big Overture *In the South*, this time to fill the greatest of all forms.

When the Symphony came, it was cyclic in nature and quite original in form. The first movement is laid out as a slow introduction (consisting of the long motto theme played twice over) and an *Allegro* made of two variants – one more distant from the motto theme than the other – for primary and secondary subjects, interspersed with other variants which keep the motto 'in the air all around' (as Elgar once described the source of his own inspiration). Between exposition and development the motto itself reappears, again between development and recapitulation, and once more between recapitulation and coda. At this last veiled appearance of the motto in the first movement, Elgar wrote:

I have employed the *last desks* of the strings to get a soft diffused sound: the listener need not be bothered to know *where* it comes from – the effect is of course widely different from that obtained from the *first desk soli*: in the latter case you perceive what is there – in the former you don't perceive that something is not there – which is what I want.

As with the opening *Allegro* in the Second Symphony to come, this movement is 'difficult' for listeners because it is diffuse. It is from this very diffusion that the final reunification of the motto and all its derivatives will gradually be drawn.

The Symphony's two central movements are based on further variants of the motto theme; but here the motto itself keeps silence. One of these movements is an *Allegro molto*. (In both his Symphonies Elgar avoided writing a true *Scherzo*, and in his plans for a Third Symphony he was to avoid the *Scherzo* again: perhaps the implications of irony in *Scherzo*-writing did not suit him). This *Allegro molto* sets a strutting march against a lyric theme which the composer himself identified with 'something we hear down by the river'. So in this movement the impulse of countryside inspiration is pitted directly against the growing aggression of Elgar's brass writing as his harmonic language moved farther from comfortable, old-fashioned harmonies. This growing aggression seemed to match the progress of the twentieth century itself. Yet in the First Symphony the inspiration of the countryside still wins out – as it must so long as the nostalgia at the foundations of Elgar's style retained its warmth. That warmth of nostalgia suffuses the long melodies of the Symphony's slow movement – which Hans Richter, as he rehearsed the work for its first London performance, compared to the slow movements of Beethoven.

The Symphony's Finale makes a gradual return to a triumphant peroration of the motto theme, showing at last its parenthood of all that has gone before. As the motto begins to re-emerge in the Finale coda, however, all the opposing moods and possibilities gather to try to oppose the grand re-entry and tear it to fragments. The struggle is short but ferocious – showing by how slender a margin the old-fashioned, nostalgic harmonies of the motto theme can still avoid the growing strife in the surrounding world as the Edwardian afternoon of *Pax britannica* through Europe turned to dusk.

The audiences of 1908–9 recognised something so vital to themselves in this music that Elgar's First Symphony received nearly a hundred performances in its first season alone – a record not approached by any modern musical work of comparable seriousness. Most, but by no means all, of the First Symphony performances were in England. What everyone responded to was the triumph, however narrowly achieved, of the old ways in the face of modern challenges of dissonance ever mounting. These audiences were the same sort of people, after all, who were to break out in riots a few years later at the premiere of Stravinsky's *Rite of Spring*.

Concerto

Elgar's next big orchestral work also met with success, but not to the same degree. It was a Violin Concerto, which had been much desired by Fritz Kreisler. Kreisler, at 30 on the threshold of a great career, had said to a newspaper reporter in the autumn of 1905:

If you want to know whom I consider to be the greatest living composer, I say without hesitation, Elgar. Russia, Scandinavia, my own Fatherland, or any other nation can produce nothing like him. I say this to please no one; it is my own conviction. Elgar will overshadow everybody. He is on a different level. I place him on an equal footing with my idols, Beethoven and Brahms. He is of the same aristocratic family. His invention, his orchestration, his harmony, his grandeur, it is wonderful. And it is all pure, unaffected music. I wish Elgar would write something for the violin. He could do so, and it would be certainly something effective.

The notion of Elgar's supremacy amongst living composers was shared by many distinguished musicians in Europe and America in the first decade of the century. Such attention was gratifying and reassuring to the public Elgar. But to the private man, each success made him wonder whether his next work could equal or go beyond. After the enormous success of the First Symphony, Elgar's music turned inward in the Violin Concerto. The medium of the lonely violin – his own instrument – pitted against the vast forces of the modern orchestra made a perfect metaphor of the heroism and self-doubt of Elgar's position in 1910.

The contrast of orchestra and solo was heightened by going back to the practice of older concerto-writing in having two first-movement expositions – the first for the orchestra alone, the second with the solo presence entering to embroider the material with reflection and variation. It was an essentially different function from the kind of central development-by-variations of which Elgar was now master: here, primary and secondary subjects could be pitted against each other, while orchestra and solo still had their roles as presenters of fact and fantasy respectively – the roles they kept throughout the Violin Concerto.

The Concerto slow movement was written first, and its dreaming reflection, with innocence at the centre, gives the keynote for the entire work. In the Symphony the mutually opposing forces could be heard as those of the outside world. In the Concerto the opposition went inward.

The last movement was designed to balance the first, with another double exposition. But the 'development' reached back into the music of the slow movement; and the 'recapitulation' reached back to the first movement. So time went backward, and the cyclic return was made a much more ambiguous achievement than in the Symphony. In the Concerto, Elgar designed the Finale 'recapitulation' as a cadenza for the violin; but the formal role of this section was so important that it could not be left to the solo instrument alone. He therefore added an orchestral accompaniment, in which the strings execute a 'thrumming' apparently of his own invention:

Rustle 3 or even 4 fingers *flatly* (not hooked) over the strings & let the sound be sustained, soft and harmonious . . .

Thus the Concerto Finale extended and extended in nostalgia, until it became the longest of the three movements.

Perhaps this length has militated against the popularity of Elgar's Concerto with the world's violinists. Fritz Kreisler achieved a triumph when he played the Concerto premiere under Elgar's baton in November 1910. But Kreisler began to introduce cuts into later performances, and in the end he played the work infrequently. More than half a century later, in 1961, I had the chance of asking Kreisler about his feelings in regard to the Elgar Concerto. He recalled pleading with Elgar to make the cadenza an unaccompanied section, and Elgar refusing (as he was bound to do if the cadenza was to fill the structural place he had designed for it).

The long Finale makes a practical performing difficulty. In most of the big violin concertos, such as the Beethoven and Brahms, an imposing first movement and lyric slow movement are followed by a Finale of lighter character. But in the Elgar Concerto the soloist, having negotiated difficult and demanding music for the half hour occupied by

**Rehearsing the Violin Concerto for the first performance,
Queen's Hall, November 1910.**

the first and second movements, then faces a veritable Alp of extended
virtuosity through the twenty-minute Finale. It is a challenge of which
many a violinist has fought shy: all too often it is announced that a great
violinist who has never before played the Elgar Concerto is to perform
it, only to find that sudden 'illness' overcomes him in the days preceding
the performance.

There is also another difficulty. Most of the great violin concertos
were written either by symphonists who were not virtuoso violinists
(Beethoven, Brahms, Mendelssohn) or virtuosi who were not symphonists (Paganini, Vieuxtemps, etc.). Elgar alone was both a symphonist
and something of a violinist in his own right. The resulting challenge is
unique in the repertoire.

The challenge was almost too great for the virtuosity of Elgar's day.
The general advance in solo and orchestral playing standards
everywhere since the Second World War raises the hope that time is on
the side of the Elgar Concerto. Despite its size, it is the most intensely
personal of all his works, where nostalgia is raised to the level of epic.

Second Symphony

The Concerto was followed immediately by the composition of Elgar's Second Symphony in the winter of 1910–11. Here the composer reached farther back into the past, to ideas which had been with him since around the turn of the century. Why did this material have to wait so long? The answer lies in the work it finally engendered. Using an epigraph from Shelley, 'Rarely, rarely comest Thou, Spirit of Delight', the Second Symphony plunges instantly into its climax at the opening of the first movement, and everything afterwards seems to fall away from that moment. It is the music of a man whose strength is with him still, but whose faith in the willingness of his world to receive his vision is no longer secure. Thus it is 'later' music than the First Symphony, later even than the Violin Concerto.

In the Second Symphony the joyous primary subject is contrasted with a secondary subject of spectral, dragging shape. So the emotional range in this music is as great as that in the earlier Symphony's first movement, and can sound in a less than first-class performance as diffuse. But here the spectres' power is in the range of emotions they open. In the midst of first movement development comes a descending melodic shape which clearly echoes the theme of 'Judgement' in *The Dream of Gerontius*. Elgar described its appearance here as 'remote & drawing some one else out of the everyday world'. Its presence at the centre of the new Symphony's first movement made the recapitulation resound its 'Delight' over hollowness, and prepared the way for a slow movement which is in its way the equal of the *Marcia funebre* in Beethoven's *Eroica*. Here a slow treading pace is juxtaposed with what Elgar himself called 'wistful colloquy'. There is no slow movement development, but instant repetition (slightly condensed) of the entire sequence of slow movement ideas. It was Elgar's first use of the binary form in a symphonic movement.

The third movement *Rondo* is the most demonic in all Elgar. Nervous syncopation and obsessive repetition chase each other through the gamut of dynamics. As in the *scherzo*-like movement of the First Symphony, there is again a pastoral strain: but now it is submerged in a terrible climax of the *Gerontius* figure, beating mercilessly through a *crescendo* which the composer himself compared to a fever throbbing in the brain. But there is no irony of the kind that informs similar movements in Mahler Symphonies. It was this refusal to regard even the decaying aspects of his world with irony that gave the keynote to the Symphony's Finale, and so to the Second Symphony as a whole.

The Finale combined perhaps the Symphony's oldest music with its most serene. Its long primary subject had been evolved partly by piano extemporising, partly by orchestral thought. Elgar once told W. H. Reed that he had only to think of an instrument, and his mind would invent something appropriate to that instrument; and Reed reported seeing the first subject of this Finale written in an earlier sketchbook and marked 'Tuba'. In the final result the tuba has little to do with its exposition in the Symphony: it had merely played its part at one stage of creative thinking in bringing this music to the point where it could 'smoothe out' all the 'sorrow' of the foregoing movements, as Elgar described it. The Finale second subject had been drawn originally out of the inspiration of Hans Richter's personality and friendship: and it was similarly merged in the Symphony's abstraction.

Second Symphony: Finale development. A more advanced sketch of the quiet passage. Elgar has inscribed it with a line from Shakespeare's Sonnet 66: 'Art made tongue-tied by authority,' because the passage sets a treble figure moving in sequences, against a bass figure repeating in place.

Towards the end of the Finale's central development section there comes a remarkable quiet passage, simple almost to nakedness. This the composer identified for the young John Barbirolli as the music which had begun his entire creative thinking for the movement. (The claim is supported by a sketch showing the simple passage in ink, and underneath it, added in pencil as a counterpoint, the figure which was to become the movement's primary subject.) Here again, as in the *Introduction and Allegro*, Elgar was showing the very process of his creative thought. But now he placed the revelation at almost the last possible moment before recapitulation. It was as if he was acknowledging the 'lateness' of his inspiration for the world in which this music appeared. In the Symphony's coda, the opening first movement theme of 'Delight' is revealed in the far distance of a sunset glow.

The audience at the Second Symphony's premiere in 1911 received the new work with thin applause, as if they did not want to recognise where Elgar's response to their world was leading now. Elgar instantly concluded that his day was drawing in, and he was right. The big symphonic abstraction whose conquest had formed the goal of his creative life was coming to seem less and less relevant to the world now barely three years away from a world war.

Questions

Elgar's friend Ernest Newman – the most perceptive critic not only of that generation but for several generations on either side – had long been urging him to heed the example of Lizst, Wagner, and Richard Strauss, and abandon the traditional four-movement symphony in favour of an extended single movement. Newman's argument answered something inside Elgar himself, for in 1913 it joined with Elgar's interest in Shakespeare to produce a 'symphonic study' of Falstaff – the portrait of a superannuated jester who has outlasted his welcome.

In *Falstaff* the growing chromaticism of Elgar's musical language at last overtook his old basis of diatonic harmony. Thus the music showed the old hero's survival into a world which would not take him seriously, and which in the end knew him not. Elgar's score follows scenes from Shakespeare's *Henry IV* plays (as he himself pointed out in an accompanying essay), but with two pastoral 'Interludes' added out of the composer's imagination. The first, following Falstaff's drunken cavorting with the tavern women, is a dream-picture of 'what might have been'. The other arises from a reference to Falstaff's visit to his friend Shallow in Gloucestershire. This is expanded in Elgar's music into another dream vision in Shallow's orchard, complete with pipe and tabor. It is followed by a sweeping rejection of the old man and all his works by the new king. A year before the outbreak of the First World War, Elgar's *Falstaff* amounted to a new and bitter showing of the composer's nostalgia. It met with no success at its premiere during the Leeds Festival or at subsequent performances in London.

A sketch for the Third Symphony.

The outbreak of war in August 1914 destroyed Elgar's spiritual world. Through the war years he produced occasional patriotic pieces and works for the stage. But in the summer of 1918 he tried once again to address himself to serious abstract composition – for the first time since the Second Symphony. He wrote three pieces of chamber music – a violin sonata, a string quartet, a piano quintet. Chamber music had been at the back of his mind for years, but it was only now that the spare and attenuated outlook of late wartime provided the focus. Elgar's chamber music has neither taken a firm place in the repertoire nor been forgotten. Always a subject of some special pleading, its strange combinations of hard and soft lines have never lost their power over a small audience. But out of Elgar's chamber music came the orchestral work which was to prove his final masterpiece, and one of his very greatest compositions.

This was the Violoncello Concerto of 1919. Barely half the length of the Violin Concerto of 1910, the Cello Concerto calls for an orchestra of the same size but sparsely used. In four short movements orchestral instruments at the top and bottom extremities of the ensemble delineate a vast horizon, through the empty middle spaces of which the solo instrument wanders up and down discoursing a language redolent of past times and past ways. Asked for its meaning, Elgar answered: 'A man's attitude to life.'

To the horror of his civilisation extinguishing itself in war was added the crushing personal blow of his wife's death in 1920. Thereafter he wrote little music. Plans for oratorio and opera came to nothing. But in 1933 he gathered his late ideas toward a Third Symphony. Enough remains to show that this would have stood in the same spare relation to its predecessors as the Cello Concerto stood in relation to that for Violin. But before his writing could arrive anywhere near a short score or full plan of the musical argument, fatal illness supervened. Had he had another year or even six months of health, Elgar would have added another major work to his life's achievement for his ideal medium.

5

Landscapes

'WHETHER THE COUNTRYSIDE makes the genius or however that may be, it is certain that no one was ever more imbued with the very spirit and essence of his own country than E., it was in his very bones. Worcestershire was everything to him – the very look of spring coming, the cottages, the gardens, the fields and fruit orchards were different to his mind in Worcestershire . . . From walking, driving, and bicycling there was very little of the county he did not know, and his memory for every village however remote and every lane however twisty and bewildering was extraordinary.'

These sentences, written by Elgar's daughter as a private memorandum after her father's death, offer an ideal introduction to one of the most important aspects of Elgar's life, and one of the least understood. It was clear to everyone who knew him that Elgar was in love with the countryside, and many people have suspected that this love wielded a powerful influence over his creative life. But no serious attempt has yet been made to explore the origins and power of the countryside influence in Elgar's music.

Seasons and Cycles

The origins go clearly back to his mother and his deep affection for her. As a farmer's daughter the entire matrix of Ann Elgar's upbringing had been in the countryside. Much of her favourite literature drew on the classic equation of the country with innocence and purity. That equation was brought to the centre of her children's lives when Ann Elgar persuaded her husband to move the family to the country cottage standing in the shadow of big fir trees at Broadheath, a year before Edward's birth. Recalling her mother's teaching, Elgar's eldest sister Lucy was to write:

She sought *natural* joy in her daily pinpricks by taking long walks, and communing with Nature in its teaching . . . She loved an atmosphere peaceful yet glowing and vibrating with her own emotions.

The Malvern Hills.

Thus she taught her children by her own example to project their emotions upon nature and the natural cycle:

We were encouraged to go out in all weather during the whole of the year. Although we honestly loved the winter we welcomed the beautiful time of spring . . . The resurrection of sleeping nature with its yearly miracle awoke.

The mother did not fail to draw her children's attention to the congruence between the cycles of nature and a divinely ordained cycle of human life and resurrection.

For a quick and intelligent child, the matter of congruence could be focussed back upon the world of his own experience – especially when his mother emphasised the value of lasting achievement in the earthly span of life. An ideal way to record a life's experience might be to find some form of cyclic expression in which to cast it – to give it the echoing form. To make a cycle means coming round to repeat some earlier statement, ideally enriched by whatever has intervened. This is casting time into a form: and the most direct, powerful, and abstract way of doing that lies in creating music without a story or programme – just music, where the whole emphasis is thrown onto the repeating of one's own elements and patterns. Such music thus follows the same form as the natural cycle itself.

Excursions

From the early years of his childhood, Edward Elgar sought for this music. On the verge of old age he wrote to his friend Sidney Colvin:

I am still at heart the dreamy child who used to be found in the reeds by Severn side with a sheet of paper, trying to fix the sounds & longing for something very great . . .

Here spoke the man whose life was lived largely in towns, searching for the free and innocent life symbolised in his own quasi-memory of Broadheath – the countryside which began on the opposite bank of the Severn from Worcester.

His mother used to send her children back to that countryside for summer holidays. In 1867, when Edward was 10, she sent him to stay with former neighbours at Broadheath. And then and there came the first scrap of dated music from his pen – a two-line 'Humoreske' subtitled 'a tune from Broadheath'. It was as though Broadheath had taught it to him.

Thus Edward added vivid boyhood impressions to the shadowy memories of babyhood and family recollection. Broadheath, with its fountain in the cottage garden, its little streams, its fields and paths, became the great good place. Its contrast with the city where the family actually lived so haunted him that the boy devised a play with music to dramatise his feelings. His stage allegory would show the gap between children and 'the Old People' by means of a stream which combined qualities of the Severn dividing Worcester from Broadheath and the Broadheath brooks:

The scene was a 'Woodland Glade', intersected by a brook. The hither side of this was our fairyland; beyond, small and distant, was the ordinary life which we forgot as often as possible. The characters on crossing the stream entered fairyland and were transfigured.

Thereby the adolescent boy reversed the real settings of his life. He moved the remembered countryside to the foreground, and put the real world of present experience into the background. It is a clear insight into his creative motivation; almost forty years later he gave this childhood music the mature orchestration of *The Wand of Youth*.

In 1869, when he was 12, another summer holiday took the Elgar family to stay in the gardener's cottage at Spetchley Park, the Berkeley estate near Worcester where Elgar senior tuned the instruments. The Spetchley cottage was set amid large pines; and the revived memory or half-memory of Broadheath remained with Edward for thirty years until it inspired the music for a famous passage in *The Dream of Gerontius*:

The sound is like the rushing of the wind –
The summer wind among the lofty pines.

As a teenager he borrowed scores from his father's shop. When he got Beethoven's 'Pastoral' Symphony, his impulse was to take it away into the countryside. And when he began to teach, his rounds of lessons took him many miles through the country surrounding Worcester. Again in 1884, seeking some balance after his broken engagement, he made for the Scottish Highlands to spend as much time as possible alone.

Some of this behaviour would be typical of many people who lived in or near countryside. But what was remarkable was the way Elgar applied his countryside experience to his creative life. Asked how and when his music came to him, the mature composer distinguished between the work of orchestration (which he did in his study) and the invention of ideas: 'It may be when I am walking, golfing, or cycling . . .' He wrote to the singer David Ffrangcon-Davies of a certain 'appalling chord' in *Gerontius* 'made probably on the golf links'. He went for long walks. This was as much a habit with Elgar as it had been with Beethoven, and also a therapy. In the midst of house removal in March 1899 he wrote to Jaeger:

I am awfully worried with this moving & do anything to escape – I *fled* out yesterday straight across country to think out my thoughts & avoid everyone – will you believe it? I had walked 9 miles & was on the road & a man rode silently (on a bicycle) behind me & said 'Oh! Mr. Elgar! Can you tell me if *Novello's have any performing right in &c. &c.*' I was speechless.

Elgar with his first bicycle, 'Mr Phoebus', *c.* 1900.

In the next year, 1900, Elgar learned to cycle. It expanded overnight the countryside available to him from his home in Malvern. He loved it. In June 1902 he wrote to Jaeger before a planned rehearsal in London: 'I *hate* coming to town – shall miss the hay making I fear. Had 50 miles ride yesterday amongst the Avon country . . .'

LXII.— DR. EDWARD ELGAR.

"THAT'S EDGEHILL—THIRTY MILES AWAY."

"NOTHING LIKE OUTDOOR LIFE. BICYCLING——"

" —OR A CLIMB——"

" —OR GOLF, JUST NINE HOLES, IS WONDERFULLY REFRESHING."

"THIS FOR THE MATCH, I THINK."

"DON'T SULK, LITTLE ONE!"

where his "Variations on an Original Theme" for the orchestra was produced by Dr. Richter in June 1899, and created an extraordinary sensation. These "Variations" were character-studies, intended to be portraits of his friends, a description which must seem to the ordinary individual as decidedly fantastic. Musicians saw in them, however, exactly what the composer intended, and they marvelled now at the extraordinary ease and originality of his method, now at his great mastery of contrapuntal knowledge, now at his great manipulation of orchestral effects.

The next year, at the Birmingham Festival, the "Dream of Gerontius" was produced, a work which Dr. Lessmann, perhaps the most celebrated German critic, singled out for special commendation, remarking particularly on the extraordinary independence of its outlook; while Dr. Julius Buths, the famous conductor of Düsseldorf, was so enchanted with it that he determined to produce it in Germany, and to that end himself translated the libretto. The success of this performance was so great that the "Dream" was repeated at the Lower Rhine Festival—a unique event in the annals of British music. Since then it has been given many times in Germany, and is underlined for production on several occasions between now and Christmas in various cities in the Fatherland, while during the same interval it will be given at least eight times in the United States. These circumstances are so unusual that England may well pride herself on the achievement of one of her sons whose "Gerontius" has been declared to be "the greatest composition of the last hundred years, with the single exception of the Requiem of Brahms."

He is a great admirer of Wagner, in whose footsteps he not unnaturally walks, though there is nothing of the imitator in his method, for it is "always original and always noble," as one of his critics has said.

Personally, with his slight physique, his brown hair, cut short, and his heavy moustache, his quick, nervous movements and quick speech, Dr. Elgar gives no hint of the popular notion of a musician, and might rather pass for an Army officer in mufti than anything else.

Musician, however, he is to the core, and if his intention to write an opera is fulfilled, a great step will be taken towards the advancement of a form of musical composition in which we are beaten by other nations of the world. Dr. Elgar's opera, if it is written, will be of a heroic or fantastic character, for, as he has himself said, "Art has nothing to do with the frivolous, nor have I," a statement which may well be believed in view of what was said of him in November 1900, when the Honorary Degree of Doctor of Music was conferred upon him by the University of Cambridge. Then the orator, after referring to several of his most important works, declared, "If ever this votary of the Muse of Song looked from the hills of his present home at Malvern, from the cradle of English poetry, the scene of the vision of Piers Plowman, and from the British Camp, with its legendary memories of his own 'Caractacus,' and in the light of the rising sun sees the towers of Tewkesbury and Gloucester and Worcester, he might recall in that view the earlier stages of his career, and confess, with modest pride, like the bard in the 'Odyssey'—

Self-taught I sing; 'tis Heaven, and Heaven alone,
Inspires my song with music all its own."

Throughout most of his life Elgar was torn between town and country. All of his houses without exception – even the big house in the London suburb which he owned from 1912 to 1921 – were poised on the borders between. The convenience and sophistication of the town was his on one side, and beckoning freshness of countryside inspiration on the other.

People walked and cycled longer distances in those days than now. Yet few made a habit of 9-mile walks or 50-mile cycle rides with no specific object. Elgar's object was the pursuit of inspiration – specifically of thematic invention. The steady walking pace that matches the average adult human pulse rate was evoked again and again in his music with the metronome marking of 72 beats to the minute. Pedalling a cycle often came close to that rate. It could provide a pulse-matrix for thinking one's musical thoughts. On that matrix could be built a sequence of landscapes composed on the borderland of consciousness – choosing this way for excursion today, another way of different familiarity tomorrow – seeing where they led, what experiences they brought in different weathers, how they led home.

Places

The majority of Elgar's mature works were inscribed with place names. Sometimes it was the place where the music was first inspired or actually written. Just as often it was a place whose distant memory was then in his mind. Almost always it was a country place. So it was that a place, or the idea of a place, became an inspiration for music. Perhaps the thought might be saved for use later in some entirely different context. However long the time elapsed between idea and use, Elgar's memory retained its track back to the original experience. Many of his works were more or less directly thought of as tributes to this or that particular landscape. And this habit of thought grew as he matured.

Two works of the 1890s had landscape at their centres. *Scenes from the Bavarian Highlands* (1895), choral and orchestral settings of poems by Alice, sought to show the romantic peasant life of the Alps. The themes were his own evocations. They made no use of folksong. Elgar was a generation older than the composers who rescued English folksong from oblivion and introduced some of the traditional tunes into their compositions. That was entirely foreign to Elgar, who once said that folk tunes were all very well for those who could not invent their own tunes. Another time he answered a question as only the composer of a *Land of Hope and Glory* could answer it: 'I am folk music.' In *Scenes from the Bavarian Highlands* he tried to be so, using distance as a focus for picturesque emotions. It is engaging tourist's music.

A journalist's portrait of Elgar the countryman (with Carice).

Elgar in the Malvern Hills at the time of *Caractacus* (1898).

In *Caractacus* (1897–98) he sought to bring the inspiration of landscape to the Malvern Hills of his home. Apparently he chose the subject not so much for its story as for the hero's identification with the countryside of the composer's own life.

In fact the old Briton had been soundly defeated by the Romans: that was no advantage to Elgar's work. It did call forth some nobly elegiac music; but the downward curve of the scrap of surviving story could not serve the heroic interest, hard as Elgar and his librettist tried. The librettist, Harry Acworth, who appears to have worked entirely under Elgar's direction.

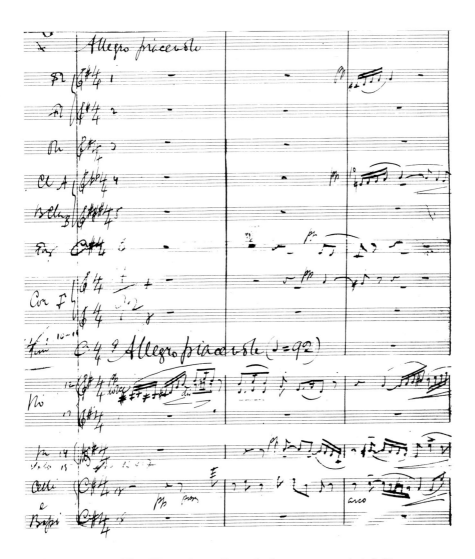

Caractacus: The Woodland Interlude, manuscript full score.

The best sections of *Caractacus* are those which show the landscape itself – in its night-time mystery at the opening, or the pastoral 'Woodland Interlude' evoking a forest near the Severn at dawn. These are set between scenes of cardboard action, because the hero can only react to the countryside and its invader. Whether *Caractacus* was the right subject for Elgar can be debated, but he would never have thought of it if not for its landscape.

Natural setting was used in a more universal way in *Sea Pictures* (1899). Here the ocean moods were so generalised that they become the collective metaphor for a voyage into the self. A different use of mental landscape, with overtones of irony, emerged in the inscription placed in 1901 at the end of his orchestral portrait of London, *Cockaigne*: 'Meatless and moneyless on Malvern Hills'. The score was written at Elgar's house Craeg Lea, built half-way up the eastern slopes of the Malverns, with a spectacular view commanding the entire Severn Valley to the east. The quotation is from *Piers Plowman*, the medieval poem in which the poet falls asleep on the Malverns and sees in a dream vision the whole panoply of human life spread before him in a landscape similar to the Severn Valley. The old poet might have lain exactly where Elgar's house now stood.

But why was this attached to *Cockaigne* and its engaging evocation of London? Probably because Elgar was at heart an escapist. Even from the Malvern Hills during the composition of *Cockaigne* he could write to Jaeger:

I am bored to death with commonplace ass-music down here – the bucolics are all right when they don't attempt more than eat, drink & sleep but beyond these things they fail . . .

Elgar's escapism, noticed by Rosa Burley, was especially associated with these years of his rising fame, when he lived in Malvern:

. . . In the old days innocent visitors to Malvern complimented him on the beauty of his surroundings and said how easy it must be to compose music there. This always provoked him to a sort of dull rage; and indeed his warmest appreciation of Malvern, as of every other place in which he lived, was not expressed until after he had left it.

In *Cockaigne* a distant landscape was evoked, and then privately questioned with an ambiguous reference to the very place he was then living – a place to some extent of his own choosing. It was not the power of landscape inspiration which was being questioned here, but the orientation of the man inspired.

Far and near landscapes

A landscape of time – the cycles of day and night – provided an organisation for the biggest work of Elgar's life. This was the unfinished *Apostles* trilogy begun in 1902. From its opening scene of meditation in the garden before dawn, the music proceeds to an overwhelming orchestral depiction of sunrise, followed by the events of the first day: the choosing and instructing of the Apostles, and the conversion of Mary Magdalene. At the appearance of Judas night comes again, the betrayal in the garden accompanied 'with torches, and lanterns, and weapons'. The first oratorio of *The Apostles* (completed in 1903) ends with a second dawn reviving the music of the first, leading to the Ascension. In the

second oratorio, *The Kingdom* (1906), come the Pentecostal scenes of
Peter's mass conversions, followed by Mary's long lament as the
orchestra behind her depicts a spectacular sunset turning to dusk – the
end of the second day. The unwritten third oratorio, to show the Last
Judgment, would almost certainly have finished with the midnight of
the world.

   In the South, written in 1904 between the two extant sections of the
Apostles trilogy, returned to earth – specifically the brown earth of
Italy. When Elgar went to Italy for the first time in the winter of 1903–4,
it was with the idea of writing a symphony. What emerged instead was
the Overture *In the South* – a combination of perspectives from the
landscape and human history of the place. The vision coalesced
suddenly one warm afternoon as Elgar and his friends explored the hills
with Roman remains above Alassio:

In a flash it came to me – the conflict of the armies on that very spot long ago,
where now I stood – the contrast of the ruin and the shepherd – and then, all of a
sudden, I came back to reality. In that time I had composed the overture – the
rest was merely writing it down.

The power of a countryside inspiration was never more clearly stated
than here. A 'canto popolare' at the Overture's centre was admitted by
Elgar to be his own invention.

   Countryside inspiration working in cycles engendered Elgar's next
work, the *Introduction and Allegro* of 1905. In 1901 he had heard the
distant singing in Wales which inspired the 'Welsh' theme that frames
the work. But this other 'canto popolare' was not finally shaped until
three years later – when another distant song, heard in the Wye Valley,
reminded Elgar of his earlier experience. The three-year gap is
interesting, for the *Apostles* oratorios were then in process of
composition one by one for the triennial Birmingham Festival, and
other works such as the *Pomp and Circumstance* Marches were also
appearing during the same years in a three-year cycle of their own. The
cyclic suggestion fitted the pattern of landscape inspiration for the
Introduction and Allegro with utter naturalness to produce one of
Elgar's most telling works.

Retrospections

   Ideas for both Symphonies (1908, 1911) and the Violin Concerto
(1910) were realised during later visits to Italy, though all three were
written largely in England. The contrast of distant landscapes helped
here as it had in *Cockaigne*, though now without the irony. In the choral
ode *The Music Makers* (1912) Elgar used illustrative themes from his
own earlier works in an attempt to marshal the entire ethos of his
creative process. The first use of the 'Enigma' theme from the *Variations*
is a landscape reference – 'sitting by desolate streams'. But it was the

final stanza of this poem which set forth something like an ideal interior landscape for Elgar's art from the days when the child had haunted the reeds by Severn side 'trying to fix the sounds and longing for something very great':

> Great hail! we cry to the comers
>   From the dazzling unknown shore;
> Bring us hither your sun and summers,
>   And renew our world as of yore;
> You shall teach us your song's new numbers,
>   And things that we dreamt not before:
> Yea, in spite of a dreamer who slumbers,
>   And a singer who sings no more.

Those words, hymning the power of art despite the mortality of the artist, expressed in terms of ideal landscape, could stand at the centre of Elgar's creative philosophy. His setting of them at the end of *The Music Makers* in 1912 was clearly valedictory.

The valediction was to the world of pastoral, countryside experience which had shaped his own birth and boyhood – the world which had waited for him just outside the gates of the old cathedral city of Worcester. It waited for him no longer. As the twentieth century advanced, Elgar was made more and more aware of the increasing urbanisation of the countryside everywhere. It was ironically reflected in his own move from Hereford to the London suburb of Hampstead in the year of *The Music Makers*, 1912. One of Elgar's strongest and most compelling qualities as a composer was his almost febrile response to the changing moods of his world. As long as he could feel that those accelerating changes carried some benefit, so long did his art look to the future with an inspiration which initially moved audiences everywhere. But as soon as he sensed that the countryside – the real wellspring of his inspiration – was in danger, infallible instinct told him it would soon be all up with his art. Every work he wrote from *The Music Makers* onward contained the note of valediction.

In the 'symphonic study' *Falstaff* (1913), the valediction is in the pastoral dream-interludes which Elgar himself let into the Shakespeare story. The musical language of *Falstaff* is the most advanced of any Elgar orchestral work. Here for once the old diatonic harmonies are upset by persistent chromaticism. There is no surcease from the driving, crackling, almost demonic activity of this chromatically twisted music – except in the two interludes of dream vision. The latter of these is set in Shallow's Gloucestershire orchard. Here and here alone in *Falstaff* the ear is allowed to rest in the escapism of 'what might have been'.

The same landscape of dreams is identified with childhood in Elgar's biggest work for the stage, his incidental music for a children's Christmas fantasy play entitled *The Starlight Express* (1915). By now the First World War was a reality. Against it, the play setting of a Swiss village in the mountains and a pine forest at night could seem as distant as his own first years at Broadheath in the cottage by the firs. His other stage work of the war years, a small ballet on the sylvan scenes depicted in Charles Conder's 'Sanguine Fan', showed beaux and belles from the world of Watteau wandering into the domain of Pan and Echo – to their cost.

The countryside emerged in a different way in Elgar's greatest work of the war years, three choral settings of poems by Laurence Binyon entitled *'The Spirit of England'*:

> Enkindle this dear earth that bore us,
> In the hour of peril purified . . .

Binyon's poems were full of references to spring and the earth renewed. But below it all was the elegy which exactly suited Elgar's music lamenting its own lost world of inspiration:

> Age shall not weary them, nor the years condemn.
> At the going down of the sun and in the morning
> we will remember them.

At the end of the war came three ghostly pieces of chamber music written at a remote cottage suggestively named Brinkwells, deep in the western woods of Sussex. The cottage was half surrounded with farmers' fields, and as the harvesting came near the house through the summer of 1918, the chamber music began. It was the result of an irresistible countryside symbolism being enacted again in this last summer of the war which had destroyed Elgar's past. 'Wood magic' was Alice's description of the slow movement in the Violin Sonata, and it described

Brinkwells, near Fittleworth, Sussex.

all the chamber music. The Piano Quintet is supposed to have been inspired by the sight of dead trees lifting up their bare branches at dusk as if in gaunt derision. Yet Elgar's chamber music is not easy to assimilate – perhaps because the changed conditions of its world are not yet entirely assimilated in the music itself.

The assimilation is masterfully made in the work that followed – the Cello Concerto of 1919 which was to prove Elgar's final major composition. It too was conceived and largely written at Brinkwells. The solo instrument wanders alone through four short movements depicting big, empty prospects. The landscape reference of this work, written so far from Elgar's native Worcestershire, remained implicit until the composer's last illness. Then he said to a friend: 'If ever you are walking on the Malvern Hills and hear this – ' and he rather feebly whistled the primary theme from the Cello Concerto – 'it's only me – don't be frightened.'

After his wife's death in 1920, Elgar had gone back to his own countryside, renting one house after another until at last he came to rest at Marl Bank, a house overlooking the Worcester which he had known from childhood. Then he reached back to his own creative beginnings for tunes written in boyhood, to make a *Severn Suite*. As he once said to his fellow Worcestershire composer Julius Harrison: 'I am glad you smell the Severn in my music.'

Elgar and W. H. Reed, 1924.

6

Practicality and Dream: Elgar's homes and finances

THE IDEA OF HOME was of paradoxical importance to Elgar. Not that he was always there, or was happiest when he was there – it was almost as if the distant idea of home enriched the farthest flights from it. That was one meaning of the nostalgia which so richly invested his music. It caused Elgar to move often, as one house after another became unsatisfactory, and to spend a high proportion of his income on the best housing he could afford. His earlier homes were symbols of his success – artistic, and therefore (in the ideals of his world) financial. But though his art wielded an extraordinary popular power for a few years, the financial support for conspicuous consumption on the scale Elgar encountered all around him was never entirely there for him. And thus his later houses tended to become sources of worry.

His Worcester childhood in the family rooms over the music shop had been humble, except for excursions to the homes of the wealthy clients of his father's piano tuning. His own itinerant teaching from his late teenage years took him into a wide variety of better-class homes, and he saw the comforts of space and warmth and many servants. Being a Victorian child of the lower middle classes, however, his instinct was never to beat his betters but always to join them.

He took what steps he could. When his sister Pollie married in 1879, he got out of the shop rooms and went to board with her and her young husband in a small terraced house that was part of a newer residential neighbourhood in the northern part of the city. When her husband's work took Pollie and her young family away from Worcester, Edward found similar quarters with his eldest sister Lucy and her husband. They had a larger terraced house off the Bath Road. There were no children, and Edward had a room of his own at the top of the house with a small piano and the chance to entertain his friends.

So he continued before his own marriage in 1889 – teaching, composing when he could, going to concerts in London as often as he might, making a local reputation as a quick and mercurial personality. The catchment area of his teaching extended more and more into the fashionable spa of Great Malvern, eight miles to the southwest. Malvern was an altogether more comfortable place than Worcester. There was virtually no industry, much retirement and financial independence. Almost every house the young music teacher visited showed a way of life that seemed more and more desirable to an insecure man.

Much wonderment was expressed at the marriage he made to a woman of small creative talents, nearly nine years his senior, and of very old-fashioned outlook. He was naturally a romantic figure, and his struggles appealed to her vague sympathies with classes less fortunate than her own. In her Elgar found more security than romance: but the place she lived in suggested both.

Hazeldine House was a country house south of Malvern, along the Worcestershire border with Gloucestershire. Alice Roberts's father had bought it for his retirement from a career in India as a Major General, and Alice had been only eleven when he died. At the time she applied to Elgar for lessons in piano accompaniment, in 1886, she had lived with her widowed mother at Hazeldine for more than a quarter century. Elgar was taken to meet the old lady, and the tea seems to have been a success. Lady Roberts died a few months later, and Alice decided to let Hazeldine. She took a comfortable house in Malvern, facing on a green next to Malvern College. There she lived after Elgar courted her, and when they went to be married in London in May 1889 Alice's lease in Malvern still had a few months to run.

After their honeymoon in the Isle of Wight, they took a short lease on a house in London, to remain until the end of July. Here Elgar had his first taste of independence. Alice had an income of about £300 a year: that was not quite sufficient to ensure a reasonable standard of living and service. Everyone had servants, whose annual wages ran between £5 and £20 a year. Even Elgar's parents in the shop rooms at 10 High Street in Worcester had always kept a servant or two, and he was never to be without them. In fact servants were always necessary, for Alice was typical of her class in being entirely 'undomesticated'.

In London the Elgars attended concerts, explored the leading Catholic churches (though Alice was not yet a Catholic), and arranged to occupy for the coming winter the large house belonging to Alice's cousins in Norwood. There Elgar began to hew out some daily routines for a full-time composer. He produced and sold a small handful of works. But when the cousins returned, the Elgars had to take a London house of their own on a longer lease – a terraced house in Avonmore Road, West Kensington. Here he finished his first major work, the *Froissart* Overture.

Soon it was evident that Alice's income alone was not enough. Elgar advertised for violin pupils, but no one in London knew who he was.

Some of Alice's jewels were sold to put off the day of reckoning. But in the spring of 1891 they reluctantly made the decision to leave the life of their dreams and return to Malvern – where he would become a provincial violin teacher once more.

Forli

The house they rented in Malvern Link was named Forli. It was semi-detached, recently built of local stone, sharing lawn and tennis court with its neighbour. It provided reception rooms big enough to accommodate some of Major General Roberts's Indian furniture from Hazeldine (for Alice was soon to sell the big house). There was room for Edward's growing library and, in a quiet back bedroom upstairs, for his study. The house also accommodated the usual cook and parlourmaid. Life was conducted with some ceremony, and the Elgars dressed for dinner even when they were alone. That was how everyone of the 'comfortable classes' lived.

Alice and Edward Elgar at Forli, Malvern Link, *c.* 1891.

But Elgar himself was not comfortable. To augment his wife's income he was forced to find teaching connections at several schools in the neighbourhood. Every Monday he gave private lessons in Worcester. On Tuesdays he was at Miss Burley's school, the Mount, giving lessons to girls whom the headmistress herself described as 'a dreary little company who sawed away to the general discomfort in distant rooms'. On Wednesday afternoons he was at the Worcester Girls' High School. Thursday was the day for his private teaching in Malvern. On Friday or Saturday he had a Ladies' Orchestral Class. During the school term there was little time or energy for composing. Soon Elgar came to hate teaching. But he would have to continue with it for ten years.

Yet in the years lived at Forli, 1891–99, Elgar managed to lay the foundations of his quality as a composer. School terms were relatively short, holidays long, and when in the vein he worked very hard – first at *The Black Knight, Scenes from the Bavarian Highlands*, and the big Organ Sonata. Alice helped immeasurably, with a domestic organisation which ran smoothly, protection from interrupters, indulgence of his hobbies even when they took him away from her, and when he was at home unfailing resourceful encouragement for every creative desire. In those years he taught himself by experimentation how to handle big musical forms in choral music. He developed his powers of thematic invention to a point where they virtually guaranteed the instant success of every major work he composed. The productions of his works were largely at festivals in the Midlands – *The Light of Life, King Olaf, Caractacus*. Only with the *'Enigma' Variations*, first played at a Richter Concert in June 1899, did he get a distinguished London premiere. But by then he had moved to a new home.

Craeg Lea

The new house was one of a group built recently above the Wells Road south of Malvern. Elgar put together the initials E., A., and C. ELGAR and made the anagram CRAEG LEA with which he named the house. This house was detached from its neighbours, and it enjoyed a commanding view eastward over the Severn Valley – especially from his study, again upstairs but now at the front of the house.

The house's dramatic position on the steep slope of the Malvern Hills was a source of inspiration. As he finished *Gerontius* in June 1900, he wrote to Nicholas Kilburn:

... On our hillside night after night looking across our 'illimitable' horizon (pleonasm!) I've seen in thought the Soul go up & have written my own heart's blood into the score.

Yet the big prospect could mock him too, as he wrote the quotation from *Piers Plowman* 'Meatless and moneyless on Malvern Hills' on the full score of *Cockaigne* a year later. And in the spring of 1903, wrestling with the problems of *The Apostles*:

Craeg Lea, Wells Road, Malvern, *c.* 1903.

I am sadly tired out & this vast view from my window makes me feel too small to work: I used to feel that I 'expanded' when I looked out over it all – now I seem to shrink & shrivel.

There was always the chance of escape to Birchwood Lodge, a tiny cottage atop the hills whose remoteness made a perfect hideaway in summer when engagements did not call him away too often. Here *Caractacus* had been scored, and Part II of *Gerontius*. But by 1903 he was ready to give up Birchwood as well. Jaeger was shocked and, feeling his friend would lose a unique source of inspiration, offered to rake his own meagre resources together to try to buy it for Elgar. But Elgar declined:

As to Birchwood: we give it up on acct. of the difficulty of keeping it aired &c. besides we are almost certainly leaving [Craeg Lea] on account of the building which will spoil our heavenly view . . .

And so, when building commenced opposite Craeg Lea, even though the plunging hillside would bring the highest roof far below his study windows, he asked Alice to look for a new house in a quieter district.

Plas Gwyn

The choice was the outskirts of Hereford, twenty miles to the west. Here was another house set midway between town and country, just as Forli and Craeg Lea had been. Plas Gwyn, rented from one of Hereford's prominent citizens, was a large block of a house, stuccoed and decorated only on the two sides facing roads which met at the corner of its garden. 'A miniature Potsdam' was the Elgar biographer Percy Young's description of it. Plas Gwyn's attractions were more to be found in its surroundings – flatter countryside than Malvern for Elgar's bicycling, and quieter roads (though soon to be disturbed by the ever multiplying motor cars). It was an imposing house in its way, and soon Elgar was waited upon by a deputation from the city asking him to be their Mayor. After consulting Hubert Leicester (by then Mayor of Worcester, one of the most beloved in that city's history) Elgar declined the offer.

He had resolved to make it a point of honour to support his family entirely from the earnings of his music. So the arrangements at Plas

Edward, Carice, and Alice Elgar at Plas Gwyn, Hereford, September 1910.

Gwyn were made. Elgar would give up teaching at last. He had done less and less of it in the final years at Malvern, and with his knighthood in 1904 it was clearly inappropriate that he should descend to such work. The basis of his life now was an agreement which Elgar had just signed, after some hesitation, with his publisher Novello. With the exception of some specified works already promised to rival firms, Elgar undertook that all future compositions would be sent to Novello. In return, the publisher offered the phenomenal royalty of 25 per cent on all proceeds for the term of the agreement. The agreement was breakable on either side with a year's notice. In the event it ran for seven years – almost the length of his residence at Plas Gwyn, Hereford – and was only terminated when Elgar thought he could make still more by other arrangements. In that he was to prove mistaken.

The big royalty was supplemented in the case of the Symphonies and the Violin Concerto by a special performing fee levied whenever these works were played. The publishers fought this, saying it would militate against performances by making them too expensive. In the end they were right. But in the heady days of Elgar's financial success, from 1904 to 1911, it seemed more likely that he would be proved right. So a single performance of one of the Symphonies could cost 10 or even 15 guineas (which represented the annual rental of a fair-sized house then). If Elgar himself conducted, he demanded an extra fee of up to 50 guineas for the concert. Novellos tried to get him to compound some of these fees, advising that he would kill the goose which laid the golden eggs.

He would not listen. The London aristocrats among whom he now moved enjoyed great houses, ample servants, large motor cars, first-class trips abroad, independence and (it seemed to him) happiness. He had pulled himself up into this world by the most excruciating hard work, excavating and exploiting the riches of his inner self for sharing with others on the largest scale of formal art. In 1907 Elgar was 50. The effort had begun to tire him. If life was fair, he should have just rewards and happiness and success and security. But life is seldom fair. He could not have inner peace while he felt the need to explore his own sensitivity in created music. And he was not yet ready to give up self-expression. The implicit conflict of forces brought him to the greatest house of his life – and moreover to the purchase of that house.

In 1911 Elgar accepted chief conductorship of the London Symphony Orchestra. The Orchestra made the offer partly because its retiring conductor, Hans Richter, had been such a friend to Elgar's music, and because Elgar himself had conducted them in his own works on many occasions with success. Elgar accepted because he now wanted to take his place in the nation's centre. Did he also accept the conductorship because of a half-formed idea that his best creative days were over? Such a thought could never be far from the true nostalgic, who as he ages habitually escapes more and more into the past. And with a past so filled with success, how might the future equal it?

Elgar with the London Symphony Orchestra

in Queen's Hall, 1911.

However it happened, by 1911 Elgar had decided to live closer to London. His wife was deputised for preliminary searching, and she spent much time and energy pursuing agents' advertisements all over the home counties while he worked at the Second Symphony in Hereford. What she ultimately found was a place on the slopes of Hampstead, well within greater London yet still poised between city and country. A ten-minute walk north to Hampstead Heath, a fifteen minute ride south by bus or taxi to the West End: the position seemed to offer the best of both worlds. It was actually quieter than Hereford, Elgar said.

Severn House

The house itself was more imposing and more attractive than Plas Gwyn, and far more idiosyncratic. It had been designed by the famous architect Norman Shaw for a successful Victorian painter, Edwin Long, R.A. Half the ground floor was sacrificed to a grand entrance hall extending across the entire front of the house, designed as a gallery for the artist's large-scaled works. Along this the visitor would pass to reach the staircase at the far end, leading upstairs to a magnificently wainscotted studio of vast proportions and exquisite finish. This north-facing space was to become Elgar's music room. In fact the grand piano seemed lost in its spaces. The studio was large enough to hold private concerts organised for Belgian charities during the First World War. But Elgar would actually write his music in a small snuggery off the main room, having a desk and built-in bookcases to house his

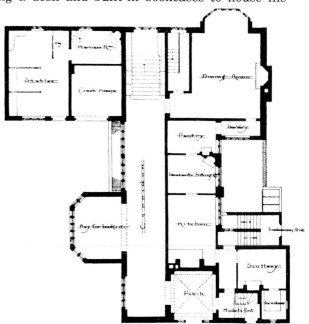

**Floor plans
of Severn House.**

Severn House, Netherhall Gardens, Hampstead.

library. A large dining room and drawing room were supplemented by five bedrooms and 'the usual offices'. There were stabling, a coach house, extensive gardens. Elgar wistfully renamed the property Severn House.

As the Elgars had always rented, they had no house to sell to provide money. He was 54 and she 63 when they embarked upon home ownership. And though his music had earned a good deal during the previous years, they had spent freely as well. The real purchase money came from a trust fund of which Alice succeeded in obtaining the capital. Elgar showed the empty house to Miss Burley, who recalled:

. . . He clearly took a natural pride in the importance of the house with its fine panelling, its long music room, and its great staircase at the head of which Alice would stand to receive her guests. But on the other hand he wanted equally clearly to make me feel that his success meant nothing to him and that there was always some lovely thing in life which had completely eluded him. As we explored the empty house he drew my attention to its beauties, but he also told me that the only part of his life that had ever been happy was the period of struggle at Malvern, and that even now he never conducted his music without finding that his mind had slipped back to summer days on the Malvern Hills, to Birchwood, or to the drowsy peace of Longdon Marsh.

As always, he enjoyed his life more in retrospect than at the time he was living it. But the future must be met. The Elgars spent a fortune on fixtures and furnishings for Severn House. When it was finished it was described thus by a journalist:

. . . One of the most striking features is the huge music room, where Sir Edward may sometimes be persuaded to sit at the great piano on a Sunday afternoon and improvise for the pleasure of intimate friends who drop in to tea. In the billiard room – billiards is one of Sir Edward's chief recreations – Lady Elgar has arranged a fascinating collection of wonderful trophies presented to her husband at the various musical festivals at which his works have been produced.

Thus Severn House was purchased and furnished and occupied in fulfilment of a dream – that hard work and virtue and success would find commensurate material reward. There had been examples enough in the Victorian and Edwardian world to suggest that the dream was still realisable in 1912, when they bought the house and moved in. But it proved illusory.

Elgar's chief conductorship of the London Symphony Orchestra was not renewed after 1913. His conducting repertoire was too small, his keenest sympathies too narrow: Schumann, Brahms, and some Beethoven comprised his best vehicles outside his own music. 'It all hurt very much,' Alice confided to her diary at the time of Elgar's dismissal. Then the war shortages left them without enough coal to run the big central heating system. Sometimes they went about the house in fur coats, prey to colds and influenza. Performances and thus royalties from his music were far down from pre-war standards. When dry rot was discovered in the stables, they were at their wits' end to know where to find the money needed for proper repair. Friends wondered how he had ever found the wherewithal to support such an establishment, and in truth the struggle was sometimes bitter. It was shouldered in large part by Alice, who wished with all her heart that her Edward might find the rewards and acceptance which would still encourage him to write new music. She bent her elderly energies to their Sunday afternoon 'at homes', when the company would include 'eminent men' whose conversation might stimulate him.

He liked it all in a way, and there was no question that he had deeply wanted it. But like so many of life's goals for which we sacrifice, the fulfilment did not fulfil. He longed for the country again. He took to making solitary visits to his sister Pollie's family in Worcestershire. Alice (and Carice when she could get leave from her war job in the Office of Censorship) again scoured the home counties for a retreat. They found a remote primitive cottage set amid the woodlands and farms of Sussex. It was called Brinkwells, and here the Elgars spent more and more time away from Severn House. It was here that his last important music took shape, while he wandered through the woods and helped a neighbouring farmer gather in his harvest. Alice was happy for him, but was secretly revolted by the primitive arrangements at Brinkwells. Here again she had daily servants to do the worst tasks. But she was bored to death, as Elgar realised, while he was 'in the seventh heaven of delight'. Once again he had escaped.

But not for long. Alice's health failed rapidly, and when she died in April 1920 Elgar was left alone to face an increasingly alien world. The lease at Brinkwells came to an end. Severn House was closed – it had failed to reach its minimum reserve price at auction – and Elgar went into a service flat in St. James's Place, close to his clubs. He was so lonely that he went to every auction and play and cinema. When he could he went to the country – either to Pollie in Worcestershire or to Carice, recently married and living with her farmer husband in Surrey.

Elgar after his wife's death with the first of his canine family, the Aberdeen terrier Meg.

Return to Worcestershire

At last he could stand it no longer, and in 1923 rented the house that was the most beautiful of all his homes. It was called Napleton Grange, an old black-and-white place lying among the fields in the countryside south of Worcester. It was largely during his years at Napleton that Elgar acquired his family of dogs. Here Dick Mountford (a Worcestershire man) was his chauffeur and valet, Dick's wife Fanny came as cook, and her sister Nellie as parlourmaid. Pollie's daughters came over to stay for days and weeks to act as hostess for their uncle, and the elaborate household of his married years was reproduced after a fashion and in a country mood. Though still desperately lonely, he grew quieter in himself. He maintained the London flat, making use of it when he went up to conduct. He composed almost nothing. But Napleton provided the balm his spirit needed; and it gave promise of better days to come.

He wanted to buy Napleton, but it was not for sale. When the lease could no longer be renewed, he spent the winter in an old black-and-white house on the outskirts of Worcester, and then went to another rented house at Tiddington, near Stratford-upon-Avon. Here he could indulge his interest in the theatre, and he kept a boat on the river at the end of the large garden. But he was still restless.

On the river at Tiddington, Stratford-upon-Avon, summer 1928.

**Elgar and his daughter Carice,
with Marco the spaniel and the cairn Mina,
at Marl Bank, Worcester.**

For the 1929 Three Choirs Festival at Worcester he took an old house at the top of Rainbow Hill – a house he had known since boyhood. It was for sale, and he decided to buy it. This was a big undertaking for the widower of 72 whose Edwardian habits of comfortable living were no longer matched by his income. His friend Bernard Shaw quietly lent him £1000. And when Elgar had duly settled at Marl Bank and was writing a little music again, Shaw persuaded the B.B.C. to commission Elgar's Third Symphony: ironically the sum they offered was £1000. By now Elgar's life had settled down to the point that he might reasonably expect to complete another big work. But soon his health began to fail. In the last summer of his life, 1933, he had a visit from 'His Master's Voice' recording manager Fred Gaisberg, who left this picture:

... Elgar ... met me at Worcester Station with his two dogs. At 'Marl Bank' were his niece, Miss Grafton, and his secretary, Miss Clifford, both unpretentious and sympathetic and with a lively sense of humour. They must have been excellent managers as the house was run smoothly and was very comfortable and tidy ...

It was an exceptionally hot day, so until tea-time we sat talking in the drawing-room, where he used to compose. Here was a Keith Prowse baby-grand piano, always open, on which Sir Edward would illustrate when discussing music. Here, too, in an old desk or bookcase he kept his orders and decorations, of which he was tremendously proud. Another bookcase contained his original scores, and he showed me such treasures as the manuscripts of his 'Introduction and Allegro for Strings', 'Wand of Youth' and 'The Kingdom'.

After tea he took me for a drive in the Malvern Hills. We stopped at the pretty little Roman Catholic Church of St. Wulstan, where Lady Elgar is buried. Nothing could have been lovelier than the view from her grave on the hillside over the sunlit plains of Worcestershire . . .

On our way home my host pointed out the school where he taught music in his younger days and the house where he gave his first violin lesson, and, what was more interesting still, many places associated with his various compositions. In the main street of Worcester he indicated a small shop where his father once ran a music and piano store . . . As usual, he stopped to watch a cricket match on the village green.

At dinner the dogs Marco and Mina had a chair on either side of Elgar. They behaved very nicely and ate out of his hand.

If Elgar's early aspiration to grand residence was not permanently fulfilled, he kept to the end the image of a country gentleman.

7

Hobbies

AS BEFITTED AN ESCAPIST, Elgar had many hobbies. Escape through literary pursuits came from his mother's example. But the notion of escape itself – escape from professional rigours into anything asking no final responsibility – came undoubtedly from his father. His boyhood friend Hubert Leicester remembered:

W. H. E[lgar] always found it impossible to settle down to the work on hand but could cheerfully spend hours over some perfectly unnecessary and entirely unremunerative undertaking (a trait that was very noticeable in E[dward] especially in later life).

In his early days, during school terms and during his single untoward years in the law office, music was the younger Elgar's hobby as well as his passion. He assisted his father at the organ of St. George's Church. He played his violin in orchestras round the city and for the Glee Club, where he was also piano accompanist. He was in every ensemble that would have him, learning music and the ways of musicians.

When he was 16, he persuaded his parents that music must be his profession. They reluctantly acquiesced, stipulating that he should apply his law-office experience to keeping the books for his father's business. This he did for a while. But his main income in the sixteen years that were to elapse before marriage came from teaching private pupils scattered far and wide in the catchment area of Worcester. He also took what small conducting jobs were offered, and kept at his composing in whatever time he could find for it.

He grew to hate teaching, as it interfered with composing. Later in life some of his friends thought he had grown to hate composing, as it interfered with his hobbies. That was to misunderstand the case. The truth is that he looked to composing and hobbies for the same thing – escape from the world of dull routine and into realms of the imagination. For effective shutting out of the world there is nothing to compare with creative activity when it goes well. But when it didn't go well for Elgar, then his hobbies came to the fore. With his typical restlessness he went from one thing to another – much as he browsed the shelves of antiquarian bookshops among widely different subjects.

Books

Elgar acquired the book-collecting habit from his mother, and it was with him all his life. W. H. Reed recalled hearing of one incident from the first years of Elgar's marriage, when he was living in south London:

He told me how once, when he . . . had been writing most of the day, he thought he would like to go out for a stroll; so, after changing into an old suit and putting on a cap, he set out in the direction of London.

He walked on and on, thinking of what he had been writing, and turning over new ideas in his mind, until he found himself in the Borough High Street, close to London Bridge, and near a second-hand bookshop. As usual, the books were displayed in rows outside the shop as well as within, and some interesting title or old specimens of binding attracted him so that he stopped to examine them more closely.

He turned them over one after the other until he could scarcely see, as it was growing dark; then finally, picking up a book he had a fancy for, he went to the door of the shop and enquired the price.

'One shilling,' said the bookseller.

. . . Edward's hand went into his pocket, and found – nothing! When he changed into the old suit, he forgot to change the contents of the pockets. He had not a penny with him. Feeling very perturbed and still grasping the book in the gathering darkness, he explained to the bookseller – whose expression seemed rather forbidding by this time – that he was very sorry, but, as a matter of fact, he hadn't the necessary shilling, nor even any money at all for that matter.

'I thought as much,' said the bookseller. 'I have had my eye on you for some time, young man: you drop that book and bunk.'

Later, as soon as he had the money, the books accumulated steadily. They were not just working books. When a fine volume on Worcestershire was published in 1895 Elgar, though still a struggling music teacher, put himself down for the large-paper edition. He bought sumptuous volumes in Lord Howard de Walden's series on heraldry. One flat in London was taken on a short lease in 1910 mainly because Elgar liked its great library, the property of the late librarian of the House of Lords.

Elgar loved to be surrounded by books: they figure in photographs of every house and study of his. Anyone browsing over the fragments of his library still preserved at Broadheath cannot fail to be struck with the breadth of his interests. Like many self-educated people, he prided himself on taking all knowledge for his province. His shelves were crowded with standard English works, old-fashioned collections of anecdotes, ghost stories, modern plays and poems often with presentation inscriptions from their admiring authors, history, chemistry and scientific works, classical lexicons, biblical commentaries and religious tracts. In 1912, during the *Crown of India* run at the Coliseum in London, he wrote to Mrs. Colvin of himself:

The real man is only a very shy student & now I can buy books, – Ha! ha! I found a lovely old volume 'Tracts against *Popery*'. I appeased Alice by saying I bought it to prevent other people seeing it – but it wd. make a cat laugh.

Sometimes he read, sometimes he skimmed and intended to read. The books surrounding him functioned as an index of what he had done and might do. They were fixed and constant companions, not subject to caprice and changing moods as human companions were. Elgar's books were the instruments by which he charted his inner life.

The music room in Severn House, with Elgar's library beyond.

Printing had fascinated him since boyhood. The Leicesters' printing shop a few doors down the Worcester High Street from the Elgar music shop offered a conjunction of art, craftsmanship, and science. Elgar's knowledge of printing served him well in the preparation of his own scores. On the one hand, he drove Novellos nearly crazy concocting one 'dodge' after another for altering plates with last-minute revisions. On the other hand, he was generous in his praise of the artistry of Novello's copper engravers and came to know them by name and recognise the work of each. It is an interest relatively rare among writers and composers.

Games

He cultivated a privileged outlook in his choice of games. His first country house visits had been to Hasfield Court, the home of Alice's friends the Bakers, in the early 1890s. There he learnt golf from Baker's brother-in-law R. B. Townshend (whose antics in Hasfield amateur theatricals are remembered in 'R.B.T.', the third of the *'Enigma'*

Elgar golfing at Stoke Prior, *c.* 1895; (*in background*:) his niece May Grafton, his brother Frank, and a young nephew.

Variations). For the rest of his years in Malvern (up to 1904) golf remained one of his chief outdoor pursuits. The opportunities for fresh air, attractive scenery, and agreeable companionship all had something to do with its appeal. It offered, as he once said,

. . . the best form of exercise for writing-men, as it involves no risk of accident, is always ready to hand without waiting for a 'side' . . . and it has the inestimable advantage of being seldom worth seeing and rarely worth reading about.

Even then Elgar was beginning to value his privacy.

Visits to Hasfield were also associated with 'japes', the inspired foolery which so often broke out among a group of intelligent leisured people during the comfortable holidays-at-home offered by the Victorian and Edwardian house party. With the young Baker sons at the turn of the century Elgar devised an elaborate charade of Royalists against Roundheads. The boys must be royal princes, of course. Elgar himself took the role of 'Nanty' Ewart, the disreputable captain in Scott's *Redgauntlet* who was a secret Royalist sympathiser. The Roundheads they stalked were any other members of the house party: Townshend and his wife, the composer Frederic Cowen, and even Jaeger during one visit – all fell victim. Elgar duelled ferociously at single stick with anyone who would meet him. The Baker boys were vastly amused and attracted. Elgar showed them an unabashed quick fellowship which emerged only fitfully in his relations with his own child.

The most gentlemanly of all games was billiards. The ownership of an imposing billiard table in a room specially designed and lighted was one of the insignia of the successful Edwardian. Elgar encountered billiards at Ridgehurst, the big Hertfordshire country house of Edward Speyer. He soon became a devotee. When at last in 1912 he was master of his own big house in London, a billiard table was soon installed in a room adapted for it. W. H. Reed was a witness and became a participant:

Billiards with Landon Ronald (*left*), Sir Ernest Hodder-Williams, and Sir Frederic Cowen (*right*), at Crowborough, August 1922.

Now, I don't know whether other people had the same experience as I had with that billiard-table; but I never once succeeded in getting Sir Edward to *finish* a game. We would get as far as 30 or 40, or perhaps even 50; but he always switched off to the study of diatoms – he had added a microscope to his *ripieno* instruments . . .

Personally I much preferred this diversion to the ordinary game of billiards: a game at which I have no skill. But that did not matter; for, as far as I could gather from our interrupted attempts, Sir Edward hadn't very much more himself, although, as in everything else he set himself to do, he was dead serious about it, and would never attempt the most obvious shot until he had thought out exactly where the balls were likely to be, not only for the next shot, but for the one after that. It was too brainy for me – for either of us I imagine, as I look back on the scene – at any rate, after these exhausting calculations, the obvious shot was missed more often than not; so the rest of the plan did not materialise; and it was my turn to take the cue and make either a *faux pas* or a fluke, after which the calculations were resumed with Einstein-like intensity.

Art

Elgar's fascination with history ran from the middle ages to the eighteenth century, and his tastes in art followed suit. In 1896 a photograph of a mediaeval carved Crucifixion in Worcester Cathedral hung over his desk. In 1907, in Rome, it was an image of angel musicians from San Gregorio. At home in Hereford the study contained reproductions of Moroni's *The Tailor* and the Dürer *Rabbit* (this a special association with Carice's pet Peter). At one time he and his wife subscribed to the fine coloured prints from mediaeval and renaissance paintings published by the Arundel Society. At another time he became a knowledgeable collector of the huge Piranesi *Carceri* prints. And he knew what he didn't like. He saw that when he visited the hostess Lalla Vandervelde, whose flat had just been decorated by Roger Fry and the Omega Workshops in a rude primitive style. By contrast, friends like Troyte Griffith and the actor Ernest Thesiger gave him accomplished watercolours of their own: these went with him wherever he lived. Among English painters one of his great favourites was the gentle watercolourist Paul Sandby. Elgar and his wife were always dedicated museum-goers: set him down in a museum anywhere, and he could be certain of finding objects which would occupy his happy attention for hours. His taste was typical of the best informed opinion of his time, and his enthusiasm was deeply committed.

Heraldry

A natural consequence of his reading, love of romance, and social aspiration was a deep interest in heraldry. He owned a significant number of books on the subject, and these he carefully annotated. He executed paintings and sketches for various coats of arms. One can see heraldic memoranda scattered through his sketches from the *Bavarian Highlands* songs of 1895 forward.

A different manifestation of the same interest was Elgar's preoccupation with orders and decorations. When he was given the Order of Merit in 1911, he wrote to Ivor Atkins at Worcester Cathedral about placing his name among the Three Choirs Festival stewards:

Worcester people (save you!) seem to have small notion of the glory of the O.M. – I was marshalled correctly at Court & at the Investiture *above* the G.M.C.G. & G.C.V.O. – (the highest Ld. Beauchamp can go!) – next G.C.B. in fact: such things as K.C.B.s &c are *very cheap* it seems beside O.M.

(Alice's father, the old Major-General, had a K.C.B.).

Clubs

A different kind of ceremony attached to Elgar's many London clubs. He had joined gentlemen's clubs in Worcester, Malvern, and Hereford. But the apex came in 1904 with his entry into The Athenæum under its Rule II, providing for the special election of 'persons of distinguished eminence in science, literature or the arts, or for their public service . . .' For twenty years he enjoyed the spacious halls and snug private rooms, and most of all the great South Library, from which many of his best London letters were written. In the midst of metropolitan noise and haste, these quiet spaces provided a perfect escape. Years later, when he successfully sponsored Adrian Boult for membership, he wrote to the younger man of 'this abode of Peace'.

Nevertheless, one of The Athenæum's rules provided for the automatic election to its membership of the nation's Prime Minister. In 1924 this turned out to be the Socialist Ramsay MacDonald. Elgar wrote to the Secretary to enquire whether it was proposed to elect 'this person'. When the answer came back affirmative, Elgar resigned his membership. It was typical of a strain of misanthropy which preyed upon him from time to time in later years – when his own music had lost the frantic popularity of the great days, and his world had been destroyed by war and death.

By then Elgar had many club memberships – the Savile, Brooks's (a special favourite, close to the flat he took in St. James's Place after Alice's death), and the Garrick, the haunt of actors and literary men. Among many Garrick friendships he valued that of Sir James Barrie especially highly. He was also elected to the Literary Society during the presidency of Sidney Colvin: he counted this a signal honour and attended the dinners as often as he could.

Motoring

Out of doors, cycling and walking were so much of the fabric of Elgar's daily existence that their association with landscape experience made them virtually a part of his creative process: they were discussed in chapter 5. His love of travel made him an early motoring enthusiast, from the summer of 1903 when he first got behind the wheel of Alfred Rodewald's vast machine which they nicknamed 'The Shover'. Throughout the war years at Severn House in Hampstead, Elgar and his wife often hired a car to take them here and there in the home counties – often to some countrified place not yet reached by suburban sprawl.

Some years after Alice's death, when he lived in the country again, Elgar became a car-owner. He maintainted a file of information on new cars, and bought one when he could. Leon Goossens taught him to drive – or tried to. In 1924 Elgar wrote to Percy Hull:

> . . . We all went to Coventry & wallowed in cars. I bought an *Austin 7* a fortnight ago for my sister who loves it . . . I was *demonstrating* in the garden & backed into a row of loganberries – they fell never to rise again.

A slight accident while driving to his sister Pollie's house at Bromsgrove convinced him that his own car ought to be under the control of someone else, and he hired Richard Mountford as chauffeur and valet. (Elgar insisted on bringing him into the 1931 Pathé film at the opening of the new 'His Master's Voice' Studios in London: Dick walks onto the floor with Sir Edward, helps him off with his coat, and retires as Sir Edward mounts the rostrum to the orchestra's applause.) Throughout the final years of Elgar's life motoring was one of his keenest pleasures. Especially along the Worcestershire lanes of those days, traffic was almost nonexistent, and the motors were comfortable and reliable. He and Dick went everywhere – to his birthplace at Broadheath, to the remote hill-top cottage at Birchwood where *Caractacus* had been completed and *Gerontius* scored, to Mary Anderson de Navarro's Cotswold home at Broadway, to Stratford-upon-Avon.

Gadgetry and Science

In the early part of the century, many of Elgar's journeys had been documented with his own photographs. He was introduced to the art of the camera by his eldest niece May Grafton, later to become his secretary for a few years at Hereford. May had been a camera enthusiast since her own teenage years in the 1890s. She took many of the best snapshots of the Elgar family; and when I knew her around 1960 she still had the glass plate negatives for some of them. Her intelligence and charm made it possible for her camera discreetly to invade her uncle's study, and through her efforts we can see exactly where and how he worked during those years. Elgar was a willing coadjutor, for he had a keen interest in gadgetry of all sorts.

A parallel fascination was the gramophone. From the machine's earliest days, Elgar took the keenest interest – even when orchestral recording into a horn necessitated wholesale re-orchestrating and

Elgar in 'The Ark', a former dovecote converted to laboratory, Plas Gwyn, *c.* 1907.

abridging of major works. The Gramophone Company of the day, seeing the chance for huge prestige, paid Elgar an annual retainer which in the end amounted to £500, to conduct records of his own music more or less whenever he chose. After the introduction of microphone recording in the middle 1920s, it became possible to record orchestral works without alteration. Then Elgar set out on a course of recording which ultimately embraced almost every major work of his for orchestra, as well as small pieces, and choral extracts from *The Dream of Gerontius* taken from actual performances. It still needed a great deal of patience to accommodate side-breaks every four minutes and mechanical problems often necessitating tiresome retakes: Elgar bore all this willingly. The result was that he became the first composer to record a great proportion of his own music.

He was one of the first serious musicians to recognise the full potential of recordings as an aid to music study. In 1927 he compared the difficulties of his young days with the possibilities newly available:

The luckier student of today can hear the finest orchestra perform the work of his choice as often as he pleases. Complicated passages, a single bar if desired, – can be repeated until the innermost secrets of a score are analysed . . . The use of the instrument for faithful demonstrations at lectures on any branch of musical study seems illimitable.

Today these are universally held truths. Sixty years ago very few people saw the possibilities so clearly. At home, the Gramophone Company kept him supplied with their newest machines and his choice of their latest record releases month by month.

Elgar spent many happy hours during his last years savouring the advances of the technology. He could hardly wait for the recording of all of Schumann's symphonies, for instance, so that he could hear these then seldom-played works whenever the mood took him. Occasionally a 'popular' record would creep into the shipment, and one of these became a favourite. It was *Oh, Monah!* by Jay Wilbur's Band, and when he sent it to Bernard Shaw this comment came back:

The perfect simplicity, elegance, and effectiveness of Monah betrays the master's hand. Have you been leading a double life as a composer? But if so, why aren't you rolling in money?

No hobby offered better escape through Elgar's middle years than chemistry. He wrote to Walford Davies during an unhappy creative period at the end of 1905:

You ask of me: well I am the same depressed (musically) being & the same very much alive (chemically & every other 'ally) mortal; keen for everything except my avocation, which I feel is not my vocation by a long tract of desert . . .

**Conducting his first gramophone record for 'His Master's Voice',
January 1914.**

After an experiment in the cellar had filled all the chimneys with noxious gases, he remodelled a former dovecote nicknamed 'The Ark' as a laboratory. He did once invent a process for sulphuretted hydrogen (one of he foulest odours of all), and allowed May Grafton to take his photograph amid chemical high-seriousness. But his experiments sometimes ended in farce. W. H. Reed heard of one adventure which he retold thus:

... He made a phosphoric concoction which, when dry, would 'go off' by spontaneous combustion. The amusement was to smear it on a piece of blotting paper and then wait breathlessly for the catastrophe. One day he made too much paste; and, when his music called him and he wanted to go back to the house, he clapped the whole of it into a gallipot, covered it up, and dumped it into the water-butt, thinking it would be safe there.

Just as he was getting on famously, writing in horn and trumpet parts, and mapping out wood-wind, a sudden and unexpected crash, as of all the percussion in all the orchestras on earth, shook the room, followed by the 'rushing mighty sound' he had already anticipated in *The Kingdom*. The water-butt had blown up: the hoops were rent: the staves flew in all directions; and the liberated water went down the drive in a solid wall.

Silence reigned for a few seconds. Then all the dogs in Herefordshire gave tongue; and all the doors and windows opened. After a moment's thought, Edward lit his pipe and strolled down to the gate, *andante tranquillo*, as if nothing had happened and the ruined water-butt and the demolished flower-beds were pre-historic features of the landscape. A neighbour, peeping out of his gate, called out:

'Did you hear that noise, sir? It sounded like an explosion.'

'Yes,' said Sir Edward, 'I heard it: what was it?'

The neighbour shook his head; and the incident was closed.

Piano and microscope: Napleton Grange, June 1925.

He was deeply interested in life sciences. One visitor to Plas Gwyn in 1907 found him conducting 'experiments on Luther Burbank lines: the netted twigs and the strange fruit he had cultivated: a hybrid between an apple and a pear.' A longer-lasting interest was in the tiny world visible through the microscope. Through the London years, microscopes often covered his billiard table. He went to the auction rooms in quest of ever better microscopes and slides. Frequent expeditions to Highgate Ponds and elsewhere brought material for the making of slides. Mme. de Navarro observed his interest in water creatures: 'He knew all about newts, water-boatmen and the like, and played about the pond like a boy.' One of his longest sustained interests was in diatoms. He confessed to Compton Mackenzie in the 1920s that the microscopic study of diatoms afforded entry into a world of mysterious and absolute beauty that 'consoles me for everything'.

Animals

Besides the doves of 'The Ark' at Hereford, there were rabbits. One special favourite, whose presence made a bond between Elgar and his daughter, was Peter the white rabbit. He became 'Pietro d'Alba', an Elgarian *nom-de-plume* for verses he wrote to set to his own music. The darkness and passion of *The Torch* and *The River* were thus camouflaged: they hinted perhaps at the suppressed passion of Elgar's love for animals. This love came to its fullest force in his affection for horses and dogs.

He had been intimate with the ways of horses since the days of Jack, the pony which pulled his father's dogcart to remote piano-tunings. Elgar himself became a passable horseman: not (as the Ken Russell film showed) in his boyhood, when the pony was needed elsewhere, but later to take him out to his first conducting job, with the attendants' orchestra of the County Lunatic Asylum at Powick. Yet he was never a natural rider, and as soon as the bicycle appeared he took to it without any further thought of riding horses.

His appreciation of horses was thereafter confined to the racetrack, and there it was lifelong. He was the universal favourite of bookmakers because he lost so often – but that never dampened his enthusiasm: at Worcester, they named one of the races the Elgar Plate. Late in life he was often to be seen at Ascot and Newmarket. Even musical sketches and programmes were annotated with racing information. He used racing talk as a defence, as the American poet Ezra Pound discovered to his cost: Elgar's stable talk put the younger man right off any further discussion of art with Sir Edward – as it was meant to.

There can be no doubt that the focus of Elgar's affections, in his later years, was his dogs. He had grown up with dogs – one as a family pet in his parents' rooms in Worcester, another as his companion in the days before his marriage. But Alice was not a 'doggy' person, and none of their households held a dog for any length of time. Soon after Alice's death, the cellist Beatrice Harrison presented him with an Aberdeen terrier called 'Merry Meg', who through her short life was a constant comfort to his bereavement. In 1924 came Marco the spaniel, soon followed by a cairn, Mina (the subject of his last completed composition, a tiny wistful orchestral piece), a larger dog called Moby Dick, and a second Meg. The animal writer Rowland Johns drew this picture of Elgar's canine household around 1930:

Whilst the great musician is writing, there sits upon his desk (spacious as the deck of a sea-going yacht), a tiny grey Cairn lady, whose name is Mina (a good name for a little dog). She watches him work with sympathetic brown eyes well-set in rims of grey hair and when he pauses in his writing and looks at her she raises herself up on her haunches and beats time with her forepaws, both in unison, as though encouraging her master to persevere . . . 'She is the cleverest dog of the trio,' Sir Edward says. 'She trades upon her sex and I have seen her chewing one bone, holding another between her paws and sitting on the third.'

So different from Marco, the black and white cocker spaniel, with the worshipping eyes and grandly-poised head, – who is really Sir Edward's very own dog and is always with him day and night . . .

At tea-time the three dogs line up in front of Sir Edward, who sits on the arm of a couch and gives them sweet biscuits and cake. At a word they simultaneously rise up like soldiers and stand at attention. A friend of Sir Edward's calls them 'The Three Musketeers' because of this trick . . .

The enclosed garden of two acres [at Marl Bank] is a great joy to the dogs; in fact, Sir Edward was strongly influenced by its suitability for his pets and the convenience of the house for them . . .

Elgar's last Christmas card contained an original fable, in which the Almighty confounds Lucifer by creating a puppy as man's ideal companion. But one of his earlier Christmas cards, quoting Walt Whitman, said everything about Elgar's affection for his dogs:

I think I could turn and live with animals, they are so placid and self contained;
They do not sweat and whine about their condition;
They do not lie awake in the dark and weep for their sins;
They do not make me sick discussing their duty to God;
Not one is dissatisfied – not one is demented with the mania of owning things;
Not one kneels to another, nor to his kind that lived thousands of years ago;
Not one is respectable or industrious over the whole earth.

With Mina and Meg, Napleton Grange, *c.* **1926.**

8

Land of Hope and Glory

I LIKE TO LOOK on the composer's vocation as the old troubadours or bards did. In those days it was no disgrace to a man to be turned on to step in front of an army and inspire the people with a song . . . Why should I write a fugue or something which won't appeal to anyone, when the people yearn for things which can stir them?

Thus Elgar described his idea of the composer's role.

One of the greatest powers of a magnetic personality projecting itself in art is the ability to survey its own apparent self-contradictions – and reconcile them in a compelling ensemble. Elgar's devotion to the countryside as a source of inspiration was nearly matched by his fascination with the society and traditions that surrounded his boyhood. When his young piano-playing abilities were exhibited before the clergy and local gentry among his father's piano-tuning clients, the boy was encouraged by his mother to emulate these superior people. He remembered especially one old house in the College Green, close to Worcester Cathedral:

Grown-up people came (I knew later it was to hear me play): also, amongst them old gentlemen – very courtly: people talk faster nowadays. And the two ladies received their friends with an old-world state that I loved to see.

For insecurity it was reassurance. For ambition it might be promise.

Elgar grew up and remained a staunch conservative in every sense. In later life casual observers never tired of remarking on his resemblance to a retired colonel: tall, sometimes fierce of aspect as he stalked through his West End clubs, immaculately attired in bespoke suits and spats to set off his meticulous grooming and elegant large moustache. All this was part of the world which he willed with every fibre of his being to remain with him and not to change – once he had taken his own fine place in it.

Elgar in court dress with the Order of Merit, 1911.

He was interested, as only a self-made Edwardian could be interested, in titles and orders. They were the outward symbols of success in a nation which accepted the achievements of its own paternalistic imperialism as the standard of civilisation. At the time he was knighted in 1904, Elgar said he accepted it for the sake of his wife – that is, to show up those of her family and friends who had 'cut' her for marrying him. He was already the recipient of an honorary doctorate from Cambridge, and as the years went on universities in England and America vied with each other to award him degrees. In 1911 he became an early recipient of his nation's highest award for creative achievement, the Order of Merit. Yet he was dissatisfied. In 1924, when his muse had largely fallen silent, he let it be known that he would accept the vacant Mastership of the King's Music. When this became his, he used his influence at Court generously: one result was to secure a Companionship of Honour for Delius. Yet Elgar himself dreamt of a peerage, and tried hard to get it. Such an honour for a musician was without precedent then; almost the last of his honours, bestowed in 1931, was a baronetcy. He chose to become First Baronet of Broadheath. As he had no sons, he was also the last.

Posterity, disillusioned by two world wars as Elgar himself was disillusioned by one, has exacted a high price for this phase of his attachment to the past and passing world. We are fascinated and embarrassed by what has sometimes been interpreted as a split. One writer has gone so far as to see two opposing Elgars – one a sensitive poet, the other a tub-thumping imperialist. The truth, as Elgar's music hints over and over in its quick turns from martial to pastoral (notably in both Symphonies' in-place-of-scherzo movements) is that the two are complementary phases of the same conservatism.

If Elgar was a patriot, so were the nationalist composers of previous generations: Liszt, Smetana, Dvořák, the Russian 'Five', Grieg. But Elgar came later than all of those. He appeared when the world of happy and picturesque nationalism (to which he responded as readily in *Scenes from the Bavarian Highlands* as in *Cockaigne* and the *Pomp and Circumstance* Marches) was on the verge of extinction. That world was the victim of increasing facility in transport, communication, and above all, speed. The old-fashioned patriotism which could grow out of the soil and geography of a specific landscape was already an endangered species, and as such it made an irresistible appeal to Elgar's conservative spirit. He wrote to the elderly critic Joseph Bennett in 1898: 'I hope some day to do a great work – a sort of national thing, that my fellow Englishmen might take to themselves and love . . .'

Elgar provided his people with several such things. The sequence of his orchestral marches tells its own story. First came the fine, nostalgic *Imperial March*, written in 1897 for Queen Victoria's Diamond Jubilee. At the beginning of 1901 he wrote down a tune so wonderful that visions rose up before him of making it the basis of a symphony, but the formal

Pomp and Circumstance No, 1:
the Trio melody which became 'Land of Hope and Glory'
(Elgar's MS full score).

mastery needed was not yet his. So he incorporated into *Pomp and Circumstance No. 1* the tune which, as King Edward VII is supposed to have said, would go round the world. When Henry Wood conducted the first performance, it made a staggering effect:

The people simply rose and yelled. I had to play it again – with the same result; in fact they refused to let me go on with the programme . . . Merely to restore order I played the march a third time. And that, I may say, was the one and only time in the history of the Promenade concerts that an orchestral item was accorded a double encore.

Clara Butt persuaded Elgar to make a song of it, to words devised after the fact by A. C. Benson beginning 'Land of Hope and Glory'. This also made a finale for Elgar's *Coronation Ode* of 1902, written to greet King Edward VII and Queen Alexandra.

Other *Pomp and Circumstance* Marches followed in 1904, 1907, and – by the special pleading of Percy Hull – in 1930. But as the new century's horizon darkened, Elgar's march music darkened with it. Already in 1901 the Irish play *Grania and Diarmid* attracted his interest chiefly because of its opportunity for a big funeral march, which he realised superbly. When King Edward died in 1910, Elgar offered to write a funeral march: the offer had to be refused because the funeral must take place too soon to permit the composition, copying, and rehearsing of a new work. The impulse may have gone into the slow-treading *Larghetto* of the Second Symphony (1911) dedicated to King Edward's memory. In many ways the most remarkable of Elgar's formal marches was almost the last of all – a *Coronation March* for King George V and Queen Mary in 1911. While nation and empire remained outwardly secure, in this enormous, dark-coloured march splendour stands side by side with anger and regret: it was one of his most prescient works.

An 'Imperial Masque', *The Crown of India*, commissioned to celebrate the Indian Coronation of 1912, contains two marches – one English, one Indian. They are written with all the orchestral skill and drama of the earlier marches but without the extra edge of commitment which ultimately gives power. One other formal march, the *Empire March* for the Wembley Exhibition of 1924, was written at a time when Elgar had lost all his faith in the efficacy of such things. It is a rarity amongst his output – a hollow sham. Elgar's real farewell to the world of military marches came in the heavy tread of 'For the Fallen' (1915–16). That introduces another story.

It is the story of how the march idiom was gradually integrated into the fabric of Elgar's most mature music. It begins perhaps with the *Sursum Corda* for orchestra and organ, written to commemorate the visit of the Duke of York (the future King George V) to Worcester in 1894. It was the first royal occasion for which Elgar wrote, and instantly his mature style is in focus: a slow unfolding of portentous melody, darkly and richly scored.

On 23 June 1904 Elgar cycled to Stoke Prior to tell his 82-year-old father the still secret news of the knighthood. W. H. Elgar was staying then with his daughter Pollie's family, and her eldest daughter May took this photograph.

Some critics have found national overtones in *Caractacus* (1898). There is the brazen 'Roman Triumph' scene, and the final chorus (whose libretto grotesquely reverses the defeat of the British by calling the future to witness). Otherwise *Caractacus* is more a study in a special brand of Elgarian heroism. That is also true of the role of General Gordon in the inspiration of *Gerontius*.

The Banner of St. George (1897) was a publisher's commission for a work to appeal to small choral societies at the time of Queen Victoria's Diamond Jubilee. Elgar made sure of one good tune for the Finale, but for the most part the level of inspiration is lower than is the case in any major work whose subject he himself originated. The same comment can be made about *The Crown of India* (1912), written frankly for the emolument. Its scoring is gorgeous and some of its ideas highly coloured, but Elgar himself could not take it seriously. He wrote to a friend:

When I write a big serious work – e.g. Gerontius – we have had to starve & go without fires for twelve months as a reward: this small effort allows me to buy scientific works I have yearned for & I spend my time between the Coliseum [where he was conducting the *Crown of India* run] & the old bookshops.

With the *Coronation Ode* of 1902, by contrast, Elgar had exactly realised the ideal of a serious composer writing for the masses. The subject was neither long ago nor far away. It was present, but drew its power from a rich inheritance. So it was a matter close to Elgar's heart, and at the same time something he could share with his fellow countrymen of every background. The musical style of the *Coronation Ode* is simple and direct, but the ideas are of such quality that the work makes compelling listening on every level. Some numbers approach the genre of light opera, but the whole design, finishing with the immensely impressive setting of 'Land of Hope and Glory', shows the composer whose heart is really in the writing of a national work. At its first London performance, the 'Land of Hope and Glory' finale bade fair to repeat the runaway success of *Pomp and Circumstance No. 1*. W. H. Reed, in the first violins at that performance, was astonished at the effect:

At the close the enthusiasm was such that Elgar was brought five times to the platform; then a voice from the gallery was heard: 'Let's have the last part again.' Quiet was only restored when Robert Newman (the promotor of the Queen's Hall concerts of the day) came forward to express the composer's gratitude for the splendid reception of his work, and to beg the audience to allow the programme to proceed, at the same time stating that on the following Sunday afternooon . . . which happened to be the king's birthday, the *Ode* would again be performed under the composer's direction.

The other face of the *Coronation Ode* of 1902 was *The Spirit of England* (1915–17), a group of three choral settings of war poems by Laurence Binyon. Here Elgar's popular style came to maturity in one of his finest works. Ernest Newman wrote soon after it appeared:

Only out of an old and proud civilisation could such music as this come in the midst of war . . . The artist in [Elgar] gives him the power, denied to the rest of us, of quintessentialising his emotions, of extracting from the crude human stuff of them the basic, durable substance that is art.

The slow tolling which frames the final 'For the Fallen' sounds a knell for the youth of western civilisation. Between the two world wars this section from *The Spirit of England* became a staple of Armistice Day observances. Since the Second World War it has fallen out of the repertory. 'For the Fallen' remains, with its companions in *The Spirit of England*, the final flowering of Elgar's patriotism in its very broadest sense.

Other war music from Elgar's pen had a more occasional purpose. There were three recitations with orchestra of poems by the Belgian Émile Cammaerts – *Carillon, Une voix dans le désert, Le drapeau belge*: they were high-class propaganda. A cycle of songs for four baritones and orchestra to words by Kipling, *The Fringes of the Fleet*, entertained audiences at the Coliseum as *The Crown of India* had entertained them in days of peace. After the war, a series of songs and the march for the Wembley Empire Exhibition of 1924, were hardly performed. The lack of popular response to Elgar's waning inspiration in this genre showed how far twentieth-century disillusion had moved from such expressions. Last of all, in 1932, almost at the end of Elgar's life, came a quiet choral elegy for Queen Alexandra, the widow of the King whose reign had seen the high noon of Elgar's creative life.

Yet the power of Elgar's patriotic inspiration, in the broadest sense of conserving the old things, underlies all the best of his music. Those critics who try to blind themselves to it are merely misleading. It will not do to confuse patriotism with militarism, closely as the two have come together in our own time.

The life of his nation was for Elgar – as for many others of his generation and century whose words and music are yet heard and read and admired – an index of hope far more than glory for civilisation itself. The aspiration marches with ineffable grandeur through the *'Enigma' Variations* finale, some of the sublimest pages of *Gerontius* and the oratorios, the 'great beautiful tune' which provided the 'motto' theme of the First Symphony, the funeral tread of the Second Symphony *Larghetto*, the phases of the Violin and Cello Concertos which give those works their manliness. As the Waltz suffuses Richard Strauss's later operas, as Ländler haunt the music of Mahler, so is the March in Elgar's achievement. It was in the end, as he hoped it would become, 'a sort of national thing that my fellow Englishmen might take to themselves and love'. This was acknowledged in 1911 when Elgar was given his country's highest decoration for cultural achievement, the Order of Merit. The significance was instantly recognised by his fellow composer Hubert Parry, who observed: 'He is the right person for it: you see, he has reached the hearts of the people.'

Elgar with the London Symphony Orchestra in Kingsway Hall, 4 June 1931. They are recording the *Nursery Suite*, dedicated to the Duchess of York (now H.M. Queen Elizabeth the Queen Mother), and the Princesses Elizabeth and Margaret Rose.

Among the guests are the Duke and Duchess of York (*seated left of Elgar*), Bernard Shaw, Norman Forbes-Robertson, and Sir Landon Ronald.

The pre-war world of Three Choirs Festivals, Gloucester 1913. On the roof of the Cathedral porch, Charles Sanford Terry conducts London Symphony brass players in Elgar's arrangement of Bach Chorales, preceding the performance of the *St. Matthew Passion.*

9

Distances

'THE SERIOUS WORK waits for Rome,' Elgar wrote to a friend before leaving for Italy in the winter of 1907–8. But the First Symphony which he hoped to write there actually waited for the double perspective of his return home in spring. Elgar's nostalgia was not only of time but of distance. Most of his trips abroad pursued the distance that could lend first enchantment and then focus.

The nostalgia of distance engendered several of his works. First came *Scenes from the Bavarian Highlands*, charming tourist music evoking things experienced on holiday in the German Alps – but realised back at home with the benefit of hindsight and distance. The *Bavarian Highlands* poems had been written by Alice to stimulate her husband at a time when his creative powers were at a low ebb. The stimulation worked, and many subsequent trips abroad were incubators for musical ideas.

For several summers during the 1890s the Elgars went to Germany on holiday, and they never failed to attend the Wagner operas at Bayreuth or Munich. In those days entire *Ring* cycles were seldom to be heard, and *Parsifal*, in staged performance, never outside Bayreuth. *Parsifal* contributed enormously to Elgar's musical language in *Gerontius*, and the *Ring* directly inspired his plan for a trilogy of oratorios. Here the contribution of distant landscapes was to help with focussing intangibles.

During the first decade of the new century Elgar's travels abroad centred on two countries, Italy and the United States. They served opposite ends. Italy he used as every Englishman since the days of the Grand Tour used Italy – as a place of dreams and visions, of escape to sunlight and warmth. He went there first in the winter of 1903–04 to try for a symphony. What emerged instead was the Overture *In the South*. It was the only one of his major works entirely composed (though not scored) abroad. Much of the music evokes the cold, windy weather the Elgars encountered during their stay at Alassio, and the stern Roman remains they saw. But at the centre lies a warm 'canto popolare' actually of his own composition, and reflecting lines quoted from the English poets Tennyson and Byron as epigraphs for the score:

> . . . What hours were thine and mine,
> In lands of palm and southern pine . . .

Italy played such a role in Elgar's musical inspiration almost every time he went there. In the winter of 1907–8, a long stay in Rome produced several fine part songs. The first, written for Sinclair's cathedral choristers back in Hereford, was set to words by Alice. Again distance lent enchantment:

> Bowered on sloping hillsides rise
> In sunny glow, the purpling vine;
> Beneath the greyer English skies,
> In fair array, the red-gold apples shine.
> To those in snow,
> To those in sun,
> Love is but one.
> Hearts beat and glow
> By oak or palm,
> Friends in storm or calm.

A set of part songs to words by English poets also sounded the note of escape in distant sunny climes – especially the opening setting from Tennyson's 'The Lotos-Eaters'. The real purpose of the Italian visit of 1907–8 was none the less the long-hoped-for symphony. Sketches were made in Rome, but the main work of composition waited for the return home.

After the Symphony was written and launched with great success, the Elgars went again to Italy, this time with their American friend Mrs. Worthington. Alice Elgar wrote back to Mrs. Stuart-Wortley in England of '*glorious* weather, the world bathed in sunshine, the air scented with flowers & resounding with nightingales'. Once again there were part songs – one a picture of Fiesole called *The Angelus*, the other a big setting from Cavalcanti in Rossetti's translation. And once again there were ideas for use in eventual major works, the Violin Concerto and the Second Symphony. Elgar even toyed with the idea of buying a villa near Florence, reputed to have been designed by Michelangelo. But it all came to nothing, like most such dreams for most of us. Elgar realised in the end that however much the flowering of his art might be stimulated by the southern sun, his roots were deeply planted at home. He went again to Italy in the early months of 1913, doubting whether he would write more music. On his return he plunged into the most English of all his big orchestral works, *Falstaff*.

America saw him for a different reason – money. He went there first in June and July of 1905 as the guest of Prof. Sanford of Yale (the

**Roman pines: a photograph taken by Elgar himself
while in Italy, winter 1903–4.**

dedicatee of the *Introduction and Allegro*). At Yale University Elgar was given an honorary degree and insulated from aggressive American newspaper interviewing. He detested the intense heat and humidity, but agreed to go to America again the following year to conduct at the Cincinnati May Festival. His publishers had urged that a personal appearance there would do great things for the sale and performance of Elgar's music in America. He replied: 'My *feelings* are dead against coming here again but my pocket gapes aloud.'

The visit to Cincinnati in April and May 1906 could not have come at a worse time. It interrupted the composition of *The Kingdom*, already in crisis because of Elgar's waning belief in his own ability to complete the oratorio trilogy. In Cincinnati he could not be shielded from the newspapers or from the ferocious midwestern hospitality he encountered everywhere. Back in New York, Andrew Carnegie extracted a promise that Elgar would come to the States yet again, this time to receive an honorary degree at the inauguration of the Carnegie Institute in Pittsburgh. Carnegie promised lavish expense fees.

For this third American visit in the spring of 1907, Elgar travelled without his wife. He conducted his oratorios to a friendly reception in New York (where he was invited, without avail, to lead a public prayer meeting against the production of Richard Strauss's *Salome* at the Opera there). When he conducted his orchestral works in Pittsburgh, the reviewer admitted:

With the exception of the applause given Sir Edward Elgar, little attention was paid to the music. The whole company was busy seeing who was there. It was the most unrivalled exhibition of local wealth that Pittsburgh has ever seen, and the best feature of the whole evening's performance was the crowd of pretty girls and debutantes gowned in luxurious elegance.

In the end the much-vaunted Carnegie expense payments amounted to little.

In the spring of 1911 Elgar reluctantly consented once more to go to the United States and Canada, with the world tour of the Sheffield Choir and its conductor Henry Coward, whom he admired. He made up his mind to a dreadful time, as he wrote to Frances Colvin from Toronto: 'Here in this awful place . . . every nerve shattered by some angularity – vulgarity & general horror . . .'

Despite some good concerts (one with the Cincinnati orchestra, trained by their new conductor Leopold Stokowski), 'I loathe & detest every moment of my life here.' In Chicago there was a murder close to their hotel, and after that Elgar lived in the Choir's special train. Near the end of his engagement, in Milwaukee, he wrote to Mrs. Stuart-Wortley:

. . . It will soon be over – *soon! soon! soon!* . . . My mind is a blank in which these people scrawl, or try to, their offensive ideas.

Perhaps he protested too much, as he was taking their money, and this time a good deal of it. But his objections were basic. On returning from this last American trip, Elgar wrote:

I sympathise with the 'good-feeling' U.S. man & woman but they are wholly swamped by the blatant vulgarity of the mediocre crowd. America is getting worse – I see it in four years . . . and we *had* hopes of that land!

Elgar was a prescient man in many ways. If he sensed, as he may well have done, that time was on the side of this newer country's preference for the future over the past and for speed above all things, then he must have realised that he would find no inspiration for his music there. Nor did he. America never really took Elgar's music to its heart, and the reason may lie in this basic contradiction of moods and impulses.

It is only now, when the United States has some apprehension of a glory as much in the past as in the future, that Elgar's music is perhaps beginning to command some real affection there. At the turn of the century, when he went there, the United States was little more than a hundred years past the revolt against England which had established American freedom. The national element in Elgar's music would have been less than easy for many Americans to take.

The national significance of Elgar's music was widely recognised in his lifetime. He was greeted as the first native-born English composer of international importance since Purcell. This was what Richard Strauss meant when he toasted the composer of *Gerontius* at the Lower Rhine Festival in 1902:

I raise my glass to the welfare and success of the first English progressivist, Meister Edward Elgar, and of the young progressivist school of English composers.

As in so many things, England and Germany were the closest of cultural allies in those years before the old *Pax britannica* finally failed. The crown of Elgar's career came with his success as a symphonist, and that was pre-eminently a success in the German tradition. Half a dozen of the many performances the First Symphony received in its first season were in Germany and Austria. As Brahms's First Symphony had been called 'Beethoven's Tenth', said the great Hungarian conductor Arthur Nikisch, so Elgar's First could be hailed as 'Brahms's Fifth'. It was not an idle comparison. Elgar was the most commanding symphonist who still wrote in the classic four-movement pattern inherited from Haydn and enriched throughout the nineteenth century by Germans and Austrians – Mozart, Beethoven, Schubert, Mendelssohn, Schumann, Brahms. Nikisch's comparison acknowledged a strong family resemblance in scope and stature as well as form. And Elgar's musical language was anything but provincial English. His style had been fully formed in the German tradition before the revival of English folksong arrived to create a sea-change in the musical language of Vaughan

Williams and his successors in the generation after Elgar. So Elgar's position was doubly paradoxical: the first English composer of international status, the last whose symphonic style was untouched by the folksong revival in his own country.

When the First World War began, there was a rush to find music which had no whiff of Germany. Elgar's popularity inevitably suffered. When someone at a thinly attended Elgar concert during the war asked, 'Where are Elgar's friends?', Thomas Beecham wickedly replied: 'They've all been interned.' Beecham, twenty years younger than Elgar, was typical of a generation turning away from Germany towards France and Italy: Beecham was the first conductor who practically made his reputation without reference to the three B's. All that came to be regarded, in the brave new post-war world of the 1920s, as part of the

In the late 1920s, Elgar joined Bernard Shaw in protesting against a new copyright bill. A cartoon by David Low.

bad dream which had maimed and disillusioned the lives of a generation – a generation more disposed to forget than to forgive. When Elgar appeared in his immaculate grey morning dress for Frank Schuster's private concert of his chamber music in 1927, young Osbert Sitwell saw him as Colonel Bogey, and saw Elgar's friends among the guests as 'the floccose herds of good-time Edwardian ghosts . . . listen[ing] so intently to the prosperous music of the master' and waiting to be carried home in motors 'large and glassy as a hearse'. A less perceptive description of the wraithlike chamber music could hardly be imagined; but Sitwell and his contemporaries saw only the man who had survived and did not open their ears to the despair in Elgar's chamber music – despair which the younger generation of the 1920s wanted before all things to put behind them.

TUPPENCE !

The audience for Elgar's oratorios had disappeared – almost as the composer's private faith had disappeared. Bernard Shaw, certainly no apologist for religion, was outraged when he attended a performance of *The Apostles* in 1922 at which he 'distinctly saw six people in the stalls, probably with complimentary tickets . . . I apologise to posterity for living in a country where the capacity and tastes of schoolboys and sporting costermongers are the measure of metropolitan culture.' Shaw was no snob. He spoke here as a member of Elgar's generation, revolted by the incursions of 'democracy' into the standards of culture traditionally the province of those who were better educated, or who like Shaw and Elgar had taken the trouble to educate themselves.

Elgar himself was equally revolted. At Wembley in 1924 he encountered the full force of the brave new world as he rehearsed the music for the opening of the huge Empire Exhibition:

I was standing alone (criticising) in the middle of the enormous stadium in the sun; all the ridiculous court programme, soldiers, awnings etc: 17,000 men hammering, loud speakers, amplifiers – four aeroplanes circling over etc etc – all mechanical & horrible – no soul & no romance & no imagination. Here had been played the great football match – even the turf, which is good, was not there as turf but for football – but at my feet I saw a group of real *daisies*. Something wet rolled down my cheek – & I am not ashamed of it: I had recovered my equanimity when the *aides* came to learn my views – Damn everything except the daisy – I was back in something sane, wholesome & GENTLEMANLY but only for two minutes.

With the post-war world so hostile to the ideals which had shaped his art – social, religious, national, and musical – it is no surprise that Elgar felt a wayfarer in an alien age. At times he professed himself certain that all his works were dead. At other times he would growl: 'The *Variations* may live.' Throughout the 1920s the lonely widower, deprived of Alice's constant encouragement, could feel in many ways that life had betrayed him.

It had not. By the end of the 1920s other voices were beginning to be heard. Even at the time of the Wembley Exhibition one critic had noticed the absence of major works for the past several years:

What is Elgar doing? – When is Sir Edward Elgar going to write another concerto, or another symphony, or any other important work? . . . He goes to revues and to Bernard Shaw plays. But he doesn't write music. He is our greatest composer and we want him to.

Shaw himself echoed these sentiments when he badgered the B.B.C. into commissioning Elgar's Third Symphony – too late. It remained for Ernest Newman, as usual, to note Elgar's real position at the end of his life. When the old man conducted the Second Symphony at a concert of British music in 1932, Newman found that the Symphony dwarfed everything else in the programme: it was as though one of the great classical composers of the past had suddenly appeared among them.

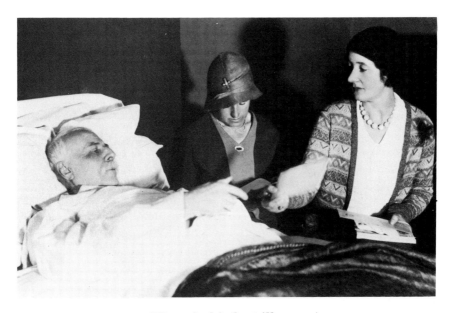

**Elgar in his last illness:
a photograph taken at his own request
in December 1933, with his daughter Carice
and his secretary Mary Clifford.**

Only a year after Elgar's death in 1934, a stained-glass window depicting scenes from *The Dream of Gerontius* was dedicated in Worcester Cathedral to his memory.

If Elgar was regarded as a classic in his own lifetime, yet largely misunderstood at the end of it, that was the price he paid for conservatism in a world moving ever faster. He was virtually the last symphonist in the classic mould and the last successful composer of oratorio, the inheritor (like Bach) of traditions he summed up but did not pass on. He has been unpopular with influence-hunters and music historians who think the *sine qua non* of creative success is a quiver full of disciples and imitators.

10

New Worlds

WITH ELGAR WE come right up against the question of art in history: to what degree, if any, does art take its value from the times which see its creation? One school of fashionable criticism has been against Elgar, preferring to make life easy for itself by protesting that the best art is entirely divorced from historical time. Such critics point to works like the late Beethoven Quartets. Yet the fact remains that the Beethoven Quartets have always attracted a small audience – far smaller than 'For the Fallen', the *Pomp and Circumstance* Marches, or the little pieces like *Salut d'amour* and *Chanson de matin* which Elgar wrote specially to please the biggest audience his art could reach.

It can no longer be claimed, as it used to be claimed, that Elgar's works are interred with the history of his time. Throughout the dark years between the wars his music always kept its hold on people of widely varying backgrounds, including composers such as E. J. Moeran, John Ireland, and Rutland Boughton. Older listeners would always flock to his works at Three Choirs Festivals. Since the centenary of his birth was celebrated in 1957, interest in his music has been continuously on the rise.

In the 1970s an entirely new generation of listeners to Elgar appeared – largely young, enthusiastic, musically sophisticated far beyond the old audiences who had first welcomed Elgar and then rejected him. This new audience avidly purchased concert tickets and recordings, making possible for the first time the recording of most of Elgar's choral music as well as new and superlatively fine interpretations of the orchestral works. The new records were conducted not only by those like Sir Adrian Boult who were loyal to Elgar through thick and thin, but by international figures like Solti and Barenboim and Haitink and Previn, whose early musical education had been entirely without reference to Elgar. This new generation has formed an Elgar Society which now has branches throughout England and in several European countries.

Young scholars begin to make studies of his music with the methods and tools of modern musicology, and a complete edition of his music is in process of publication.

What has happened, and what does it mean? To answer those questions fully would be to write the history of the world in the second half of the twentieth century – a history not yet complete. In the end, there is no better guide to one's world than one's own responses. Though I am older than some of the young Elgarians and my enthusiasm for his music is older, I am on their side. When Elgar's music first reached my teenage ears around 1950, it brought hints of promise, of unselfishness and vision to a world of darkening experience. To my young life, shadowed by the distant disasters of the Second World War, disheartened by the hard economies needed to realise metallic promises of 'success', this music seemed to breathe an atmosphere where human values and private virtues counted in a way I had hardly met with before then. I already knew and loved a wide range of music; but nothing except Bach and Handel began to answer me as Elgar did. Ultimately my responses to his music opened many further doors to both music and friendships which have enriched my life beyond calculation. This experience is shared by many friends similarly devoted to Elgar's music.

Such an ability to touch dreams on different levels of musical sophistication, and to 'reach the hearts of the people', places Elgar in a strange historical position. On the one hand, you can meet with his music in situations to which hardly any other serious older composer in the entire history of the art could penetrate – as I did one morning last summer. From my garden I watched a builder's assistant working on the roof of a cottage, and heard him whistling *Chanson de matin* amid a wide variety of popular fare – over and over, quite unconscious of its august origin, concerned only with its sheer quality of musical impulse. On the other hand, pursuing my interest in Elgar during several years in American academic circles, I have more than once been challenged by the deliberate gritty rudeness of: 'Why don't you find a first-rate composer?' – a remark invariably based on real ignorance of Elgar's large works and distrust of such popular success as *Land of Hope and Glory*. You might hear less of that nowadays. But the jealousy and malice are still there, below the surface. In England it takes the form of Oxbridge-accented superiority to anything English which has the effrontery to arrogate Beethovenish powers to itself.

These voices have been with Elgar's music for a long time now, and I do not look for them to disappear soon. It is as though the Anglo-Saxon world distrusts any such attempt to bring its own musical dreams so close to realisation at home, to entwine them so closely with its own history and soil. It is an attitude one never encounters in the much more musically chauvinistic nations – France, Germany, Italy, the small countries of central Europe, and Russia. Those cultures – far more musically provincial than the cosmopolitan attitudes revealed in the concert programmes of London, New York, or Chicago – seem happier with music that is 'closer to home'. None have the broad and truly international spectrum of the British and American orchestras and choral societies regularly available in their active repertoires. I have sometimes been approached by a continental listener (never by a professional musician) with the question: 'Who is Elgar? How can he be of importance since we do not have his music in our programmes here?' My reply is: 'That is because your programmes are more limited and more provincial than ours.'

It is true, but it does not entirely answer the question of why Elgar's music does not so easily travel abroad. There is doubtless something in the music itself which deeply touches its devotees, but limits in some degree its universality. What this limiting quality may be is difficult for me to say, as it doesn't strongly affect me. But I have an idea about where to look for it. I would look first in the national overtones in which many people today can hardly help hearing hints of political aggression – and no wonder. But the years of bad experience for the oldest generation now alive only just overlap the years of Elgar's experience, and what depresses them depressed him. In March 1933, less than a year before his death, he wrote to Frank Schuster's sister Adela:

I am in a maze regarding events in Germany – what are they doing? In this morning's paper it is said that the greatest conductor Bruno Walter &, stranger still, Einstein are ostracised: are we all mad? The Jews have always been my best & kindest friends – the pain of these news is unbearable & I do not know what it really means.

Even Elgar's nationalistic music sings of a world in which security and virtue and peace are at least reasonable dreams, even if closely surrounded and pursued by spirits of negation. Many people nowadays find it difficult to accept anything but blackness and irony as honest expression.

And there is another negative force, for long operative in America and appearing more and more in Britain. This is speed – concern with 'getting there' within the fewest minutes or hours or years, and 'saving time' for a future that fewer and fewer really want to face. For this haunted, driven sort of spirit, the glow at the centre even of Elgar's darkest music is antipathetic in a way the lengthy acerbities of Wagner and Mahler are not. And these hard ironies are likely to persist as far beyond 1984 as anyone now can foresee. To the extent that they persist, they will limit the audience for Elgar's best music.

Yet there is one mighty force operating on the other side. For the first time in history, the whole art of 'classical' music today is not modern: the basis of its performing repertory is not anchored in its own time. This was not true of any previous century, and some have predicted the death of music in the museums. Fortunately concert and opera receipts show no sign whatever that the people of 1984, of any political stripe, regard the music of the past as irrelevant to them. And the greatest following of all is for music of the nineteenth century – the great century of music, which produced the greatest number of composers who can still reach the hearts of the people. The continued ability of Elgar's music to do this, in the face of the all but complete disappearance of the trappings of his world, is proof positive that his music contains the eternities which continue to give it immortality. Chief among all these qualities, I think, is its atmosphere of countryside innocence. It was a worker in my world, after all, who whistled *Chanson de matin* as he repaired an old roof against the storms of the 1980s and beyond.

The Elgar Birthplace as it looks today.

Record List

All recordings played and conducted by Elgar himself known to survive (with one exception – *Serenade Mauresque*, still awaiting release) have been reissued in LP form. Record numbers are of the last known form of release, and are not necessarily still in the catalogues. All Pearl GEM records are of acoustic process recordings of limited fidelity. The Pearl Opal and all EMI records are of electric process recordings, which should give good sonic results for their age.

Abbreviations
BBCSO – B.B.C. Symphony Orchestra
LPO – London Philharmonic Orchestra
LSO – London Symphony Orchestra
NSO – New Symphony Orchestra
Phil Chr – Philharmonic Orchestra
RAHO – Royal Albert Hall Orchestra
SO – Symphony Orchestra
Full details and histories of all these recordings will be found in the author's previous book *Elgar on Record*, available only from the Elgar Birthplace Museum, Broadheath, Worcester.

Banner of St. George, The: Epilogue
   Philharmonic Choir, LSO EMI RLS 713
Bavarian Dances, Three (orchestration of *Scenes from the Bavarian Highlands*)
   SO (1914–17) Pearl GEM 113
   LSO (1927–32) EMI RLS 713
Beau Brummel: Minuet
   LSO (1928) EMI RLS 713
   NSO (1929) EMI RLS 713
Caractacus: extracts (rec. supervised by Elgar)
   LSO/Collingwood EMI RLS 713
Carillon: Henry Ainley
   SO Pearl GEM 112
Carissima:
   SO (1914) Pearl GEM 111
Chanson de matin:
   LSO EMI RLS 713

Chanson de nuit:
  SO (1919) Pearl GEM 113
  RAHO (1926) EMI RLS 713
Civic Fanfare and National Anthem:
  3 Choirs Festival 1927 EMI RLS 708
Cockaigne: Overture
  RAHO (1926) EMI RLS 713
  BBCSO (1933) EMI RLS 713
  – *abr.* SO (1917) Pearl GEM 111
Concerto, Violin. Menuhin
  LSO (1932) EMI RLS 708
  – *abr.* Hall, SO (1916) Pearl GEM 112
Concerto, Violoncello
  Harrison LSO (1928) EMI RLS 708
  – *abr.* Harrison, SO (1919) Pearl GEM 113
Contrasts:
  LPO EMI RLS 713
Crown of India, The: Suite
  LSO EMI RLS 713
Dream of Gerontius, The: Prelude and extracts.
  Royal Choral Soc. 1927 Pearl Opal 810
  Extracts. Royal Choral Soc. 1927 EMI RLS 713
  Extracts. 3 Choirs Festival 1927 EMI RLS 708
  Prelude and Angel's Farewell (*abr.*) (1917) Pearl GEM 111
Elegy:
  LPO EMI RLS 713
'Enigma' Variations:
  SO (1920–21) Pearl GEM 114
  RAHO (1926) EMI RLS 708
Falstaff:
  EMI RLS 708
  – Interludes. EMI RLS 713
Fringes of the Fleet, The:
  Mot, Stewart, Henry, Barratt, SO Pearl GEM 112
Froissart Overture
  LPO EMI RLS 713
In the South Overture
  RAHO (1921–23) Pearl GEM 115
  LSO (1930) EMI RLS 713
Kingdom, The: Prelude
  BBCSO EMI RLS 708
King Olaf: A little bird in the air
  – *abr.* RAHO Pearl GEM 114
Land of Hope and Glory
  Balfour, Phil. Chr, LSO (1928) EMI RLS 713
  LSO (Pathé sound-track, 1931) EMI RLS 713
Light of Life, The: Meditation
  RAHO (1925) Pearl GEM 116
  RAHO (1926) EMI RLS 713
May Song:
  NSO EMI RLS 713
Mazurka:
  NSO EMI RLS 713
Minuet Op. 21
  NSO EMI RLS 713

Music Makers, The: extracts
  3 Choris Festival 1927 EMI RLS 708
National Anthem: arrgt.
  Phil Chr LSO EMI RLS 713
Nursery Suite:
  LSO EMI RLS 713
Piano Improvisations:
  EMI RLS 713
Polonia
  – *abr.* SO Pearl GEM 113
Pomp and Circumstance: Marches
  No. 1. RAHO (1926) EMI RLS 713
        BBCSO (1932) EMI RLS 713
        – *abr.* SO (1914) Pearl GEM 110
  No. 2. RAHO (1926) EMI RLS 713
        BBCSO (1932) EMI RLS 713
  No. 3. LSO EMI RLS 713
  No. 4. SO (1914) Pearl GEM 110
        LSO (1927) EMI RLS 713
        BBCSO (1933) EMI RLS 713
  No. 5. LSO EMI RLS 713
Rosemary:
  NSO EMI RLS 713
Salut d'amour:
  SO (1914) Pearl GEM 110
  NSO (1929) EMI RLS 713
Sanguine Fan, The: extracts
  SO Pearl GEM 114
Sea Pictures: Megane,
  SO Pearl GEM 115
Serenade for Strings:
  LPO EMI RLS 713
Sérénade Lyrique:
  NSO EMI RLS 713
Severn Suite:
  LSO EMI RLS 713
Starlight Express, The: extracts
  Nicholls, Mott, SO Pearl GEM 111
Symphony No. 1
  LSO EMI RLS 708
Symphony No. 2
  RAHO (1924) Pearl GEM 116
  LSO (1927) EMI RLS 713
Wand of Youth, The: Suites 1 and 2
  LSO EMI RLS 713
  – extracts. SO (1917–19) Pearl GEM 110

Works by Other Composers
Bach: Fantasia and Fugue in C minor (arr. Elgar)
  RAHO (1921–23) Pearl GEM 115
  RAHO (1926) EMI RLS 708
Croft: *O God Our Help in Ages Past*
  Phil Chr, LSO EMI RLS 713
Handel: Overture in D minor (arr. Elgar)
  RAHO Pearl GEM 115

Index

Elgar's works are indexed alphabetically under the composer's name.